TEN CHRISTIANS

By their deeds you shall know them:

TEN CHRISTIANS

Boniface Hanley, O.F.M.

AVE MARIA PRESS

Notre Dame, Indiana 46556

Acknowledgments

I depended heavily upon the skills and talents of many in the publication of *Ten Christians*.

I am particularly indebted to the staff of St. Anthony's Guild, Paterson, New Jersey. The Guild's Director, Father Salvator Fink, O.F.M., not only selected the subjects of these sketches, but encouraged me to meet the deadlines for each of them. Guild staff members, Father John J. Manning, O.F.M., carefully researched our subjects and Mary Alice Slater did painstaking editorial work.

I also wish to express my appreciation to Doris Dooren and Elizabeth Ann Crocker, who not only prepared the manuscripts for publication, but also offered gracious and pointed criticisms of them.

To Father Roy Gasnick, O.F.M., Director of the Franciscan Communications Office in New York City and Mr. James Conniff, President of Megadot, Inc., Upper Montclair, New Jersey, I owe a special word of thanks for their perseverance in bringing this book to publication.

But most of all I must express my gratitude to my Franciscan confreres who listened patiently to my endless chatter about the people of whom I write. It was my fellow friars who encouraged me to bring this work to the wider audience I hope it will now have.

Father Boniface Hanley, O.F.M.

Contents

Author's Foreword 9

1. Pierre Toussaint 15

2. Damien De Veuster 39

3. Frederic Ozanam 67

4. Maximilian Kolbe 93

5. Teresa of Calcutta 119

6. St. Francis of Assisi 141

7. St. John Bosco 165

8. Rose Hawthorne Lathrop 195

9. Joseph Cardinal Cardijn 217

10. St. Therese of Lisieux 245

Author's Foreword

This book is dedicated to people-watching, though we hope the reader will do more than watch the 10 persons he will encounter in these pages. They are 10 people worth knowing well.

Each of them experienced the confusion, disappointments, the pain and frustration that are the lot of all of us. Yet under the impact of suffering they grew more profoundly human, their love of life expanded and deepened, their belief in the goodness of God and their fellowman took firmer root in their hearts.

Some participated in major historical events; others lived in such obscurity that only chance (or was it Providence?) preserved the memory of their lives and deeds.

Regardless of the time or circumstances of their lives, all these people share a common calling. They are teachers. And the course they teach could be entitled "How to Live—Now." Each of our 10 modelled his or her life on the Way of Life taught by Christ, the one Teacher. In this they teach us nothing new—their doctrine is Christ's doctrine. The "Now" part of the course title, however, indicates the special contribution of each one. For it was their mission to apply the Gospel truths to the concrete circumstances of their lives.

Jesus, as we know, taught his Way of Life in a specific place and time in human history. He spoke words and cited examples men and women of his day readily understood. The universal truth of Jesus' message, however, requires translation into languages and examples men of other times and cultures can grasp. For this reason the Lord established the church and charged it with the duty to "teach all men."

Not surprisingly the 2000-year history of the church has proved her most effective teachers are the people who struggle to understand Christ's teachings and live them without compromise. These people belong, of course, to a particular place, specific time and culture in history, and thus adapt the gospel teaching to circumstances their contemporaries readily understand.

For instance, we who have witnessed the power of the media to destroy reputations can appreciate a Don Bosco who forgave from his heart the journalists who vilified him in Italy's anticlerical press. Bosco's tolerance and refusal to seek revenge provide a clear example to us of what Christ meant when he said, "Forgive your enemies, do good to those who harm you."

We can also appreciate the near despair a woman like Rose Hawthorne experienced as she failed again and again in her efforts to help her husband overcome his addiction to alcohol.

After his untimely death, Rose, instead of yielding to bitterness and anger, turned to help victims of cancer. We all know about cancer and alcoholism. Rose Hawthorne teaches us how a Christian deals with both.

There are saints like Francis of Assisi whose genius breaks through the barriers of time and place and culture. In clearest language Francis demonstrates to men and women of every generation what the presence of God in all creation truly means. He sings to Brother Sun and Sister Moon; he preaches to birds, rabbits, and insects and patiently teaches a rowdy wolf decent manners. Nobody, man, woman or child, can fail to understand Francis' message—that is why he is called "Everybody's Saint." Universal teachers like Francis are rare, however, even in the catalog of the saints. Most saints are more limited in their appeal. But all saints and holy people are accepted as teachers because by the manner of their lives they prove it is possible for human beings to live the Gospel of Christ.

It is precisely because they are human that the saints are credible. Unfortunately traditional biographers of the saints and holy people (called hagiographers) have not always accepted this principle. Indeed, before the advent of scientific historical research little more than a century ago, hagiographers tended to emphasize the miraculous and ignore the human aspects of their saints' history.

In so doing they were only following the patterns established by storytellers and legend-makers throughout the ages. These guardians of tradition communicated the extraordinary qualities of their tribe or nation's heroes by exaggerating certain details of their lives. As late as the 19th century Americans were delighted to hear how George Washington bravely acknowledged to his father that he had, indeed, cut down the cherry tree. Such stories stress the honesty and strength of the father of our country. That George possessed such qualities few will deny; few will agree that he possessed them to the extent the legends suggest.

Here of course lies the weakness of the storytelling method of history—or hagiography. The subject's true self is very often buried by the legend. Hagiographers focusing on the miraculous may prove their saint shares God's powers and is therefore holy. They often do this, however, at the expense of obscuring the true personality and human limitations of their subject.

We are all familiar, for instance, with St. Patrick's marvelous deed of driving the snakes out of Ireland. Do we know, however, that in his youth Patrick commited a sin so grave (perhaps murder) that he fell under the church's public censure? His conscience troubled him for years (even after he became a bishop) because of his crime.

St. Anthony of Padua's biographers note that Anthony could be in two places at the same time (for instance Portugal and Italy) cheerfully performing miracles in both. But the storytellers say little about the anguish Anthony experienced when he left the Augustinian Order to join the Franciscans.

Unfortunately, emphasizing the "miraculous" and downplaying the human separated the saint from the rest of us. We put the saint on a pedestal, stripped of precious humanity.

Recent hagiography, profiting from new methods of writing history, takes a more balanced view. The particular personality of the saint or venerated person becomes important because it profoundly influences the person's life-style and his approach to Christ.

Thus hagiographers are now revealing both the strong and weaker elements of the saint or holy person's character. Who can deny the courage of a man like Maximilian Kolbe who surrenders his life for another at Auschwitz; or a Damien De Veuster who enters the doors of death to serve the lepers at Molokai, or Pierre Toussaint who remains in New York City to hunt for plague victims when others flee? At the same time we must know that Damien De Veuster almost lost his nerve the first few days at Molokai; that Pierre Toussaint was a man so much in love with his wife that when she died he almost came apart; that Maximilian Kolbe felt the harsh misjudgments of his religious superiors very keenly.

Some of our 10 subjects have been "canonized." The church has officially approved their lives, stated they have reached heaven and holds them up to us as examples of Christian living. Some of our profiles concern people who are not canonized; indeed one is still living.

The canonization process as we all know has often been sparked by political pressures, national needs or the promotion of a religious order. But this does not alter the fact that the people canonized are worthy of the honor. What is unfortunate is that many people worthy of the honor will never receive it and we will know nothing of their lives because there is no organization to promote their cause. And the church is the poorer for that.

I began writing sketches of the saints and holy people eight years ago when Father Salvator Fink, O.F.M., director of St. Anthony's Guild, Paterson, New Jersey, asked me to join him in producing the Guild's quarterly magazine The Anthonian. We decided then to use modern photojournalistic techniques to tell the stories of people close to our times who lived the gospel. The venture was an immediate success as the mail of our readers testified. Although we are proud of our work with The Anthonian we realize it isn't the technique that makes the magazine popular; it is the content. Modern saints and holy people have something to say to all of us; something we need to hear and understand. Our hope is that the readers of this book will profit from this meeting with our 10. We feel certain they will, for it remains as true today as when the Sage wrote it thousands of years ago—"How beautiful you are, O Lord, in your holy people."

1. Pierre Toussaint

It was a cool autumn evening in New York. The sun had set an hour earlier. A shower of bright, gentle light cascaded from a harvest moon that hung, a luminous white disc, in the blue-black skies that arched overhead. The lamplighter, moving steadily on his rounds, touched his wand to the gas lamps that now added a soft, subtle glow to the city streets.

Only the "clop-clop" of horses' footfalls, the creaking of carriages on the unpaved avenues and the greetings that neighbors called to one another broke the quiet of the evening.

Along a narrow street called Reade, a tall, lithe man, clad in a greatcoat and a three-cornered hat, walked rapidly through the night. Entering a three-story home on the street, he mounted the stairs and halted at the second floor. He tapped gently on the door.

"Madame," he asked in French, "may I come in?"

"Yes," the voice from inside responded. It was a tired voice.

Entering and throwing off his coat, the man sat for a moment in a chair. Then he bent over and lighted the small oil lamp on a table near a chair in which Madame was resting. The glow of the lamp illumined

The production of indigo dye was an economic mainstay in the French colony of Haiti, as well as refining sugar. Thousands of blacks were slave workers on these plantations.

her face and figure. She was in her middle 30s. Her features, delicate and refined, hinted accurately at her aristocratic origins. Her eyes, lifeless, apprehensive, mirrored the tragedy that haunted her. Life had struck this formerly gay young lady one cruel blow after another. Twice widowed at 30, she had experienced exile, financial ruin and mental shock. Now her physical health was failing. There are people who grow strong under suffering. Madame Marie Elisabeth Nicolas was not one of these.

The tall gentleman offered the lady a package.

"Please, Madame, try one of these bonbons. They are good, and you will enjoy them." His voice was musical, gentle. The amber glow from the oil lamp washed over his face. It was a face full of kindness. His dark eyes and fine mouth manifested force of character. He was a black man, a hairdresser by trade, and his name was Pierre Toussaint.

Pierre's story begins in Saint Domingue (present-day Haiti) in 1766, a decade before the American Revolution. In those days Haiti, France's wealthiest Caribbean colony, produced sugar, coffee, indigo, tobacco and fruit in such profusion and abundance that two-thirds of all French commerce was conducted with the island. Any enterprising Frenchman who invested heavily in a Haitian plantation could earn a huge fortune in as few as three years.

French plantation owners, relatively few in number, formed the top of a pyramid of wealth that rested on the bent backs of thousands of African slaves. Seven hundred thousand blacks toiling under a merciless Caribbean sun provided wealth beyond imagination for their French masters. Owners kept the slaves under control by merciless discipline. Rebellious or even disorderly slaves were brutalized. Beaten to death in the fields, burned

The slightest mistake brought 20 lashes with the whip. The working life expectancy of a slave was seven years.

at the stake, crucified, drowned, mutilated, slashed and scourged, blacks were kept in terror of their owners. The whip crack, it was said, was Haiti's characteristic sound.

Although the French king had established policies to safeguard basic justice for blacks, in practice colonial administrators combined with the wealthy French planters to oppress the slaves. French planters who treated slaves with even minimal Christian respect were considered by their peers to be threats to the security of the island.

There were a few planters, nevertheless, who refused to bow under the pressure of their fellow plantation owners. One was a certain Monsieur Jean Berard, owner of a large plantation in northern Haiti. Berard treated his slaves with genuine respect. One of them, a young black named Pierre Toussaint, he encouraged to read and write and to explore the treasures of the extensive Berard library.

French planters, gorged with wealth, were unable or unwilling to sense the winds of deadly fury gathering about Haiti. At night, voodoo drums beat their deadly rhythms. Slaves slipped from plantations into the island's dark glens and hidden grottoes to join in the secret rituals.

Participating in animal sacrifice and drinking a potent brew of animal blood mixed with rum and gunpowder, the worshipers chanted this prayer:

> The God who created the sun, which gives us light, who rouses the waves and rules the storm, though hidden in the clouds, he watches us.
>
> He beholds the misdeeds of the whites.
>
> The white man's god inspires him with crime; our God calls upon us to do good works.
>
> But, though our God is merciful, he wishes us to be avenged.
>
> He will direct our arms and aid us.
>
> Throw away the symbol of the god of the whites, that god who gloats over our suffering, and listen to the voice of liberty, which finds an echo in our hearts.

As they prayed, the devotees danced and whipped themselves into a religious frenzy. With exhaustion came peace. With waiting came new resolves to destroy their tormentors.

New York hairdressers created lavish styles and refurbished wigs for both men and women.

If Pierre Toussaint as a youth knew of these secret rites, and most likely he did, we have no record of his joining in them. His grandmother and mother were devout Catholics, as was his master, Monsieur Berard. Pierre, intelligent and cheerful, was deeply rooted in the Catholic faith. He grew tall, slim, and graceful in mind and manner. Berard assigned him to work in the plantation's great house. Thus, Toussaint was spared the harsher life of the field hand and the bitterness it engendered.

In the mid-1780's, Jean Berard, himself a widower, married a young widow, Marie Elisabeth Bossard Roudanes, an aristocratic daughter of a wealthy French planter. Jean had a premonition that the hurricane of black retaliation, so long forming, was about to burst over Haiti. He decided to move his new wife, his two sisters, a retinue of servants and himself to New York City to wait out the storm. In the Berard party were Pierre and Pierre's sister, Rosalie.

Pierre sought news from Haiti on the busy South Street docks.

By the late 1780's, New York was the capital of the new American nation. The city hosted George Washington's inauguration as first President of the United States. The father of our country lived at No. 3 Cherry Street. Most of New York's 30,000 citizens dwelt near the waterfront. Some adventurous families lived on the northern rim of the city in a suburb called Greenwich Village. The Jays, the Washingtons, and other New York first families carried on an active social life.

Americans, still basking in the glow of their victory over the British and their newly won independence, were full of confidence in their future. Yankee gratitude flowed readily to the French, who had dramatically and effectively assisted Washington in his decisive defeat of General Cornwallis at Yorktown in 1781. New Yorkers welcomed and respected the members of the small French colony who had settled among them. It was this group of Frenchmen that Monsieur Berard and his family joined.

Before leaving Haiti, Berard had arranged to rent a home on New York's Reade Street. Soon after settling in the house, his master enlisted Pierre as an apprentice to a Mr. Merchant, one of the city's leading hairdressers. The young slave, intelligent and deft, made rapid progress under Merchant's careful training. Pierre had genuine talent for the complicated art of coiffure. The day's hair styles were most elaborate; hairdressers' fees were substantial. It was not unusual for a lady of fashion to spend $1,000 yearly on the care and dressing of her hair. It was no small amount when we remember that a man who had an income of $10,000 a year was considered wealthy.

Pierre brought both skill and a unique personality to his work. Courteous, kind, and cheerful, Pierre attracted people. His quiet wit and gaiety lifted the spirits of those about him. It was not long before he had many customers.

Members of the Berard household took it for granted that, as soon as the troubles in Haiti were over, the family would return. Jean Berard brought only enough funds to maintain his family comfortably for a year in New York.

News from Haiti, however, was scarce in coming. What little did leak through was all bad. Premonitions of serious trouble grew among New

York's Frenchmen, many of whom had family and financial interests in Haiti. Rumors and uncertainty grew too much for Jean Berard. He decided to return to Haiti to look to his plantation.

Haiti's bloody ferment was coming to a boil as Monsieur Berard returned. The terror, fear and mutual hatred that infected all levels of the island's society exploded in an orgy of vicious crime and reprisal. Blacks had discovered a new weapon which they wielded with ease. Haiti's great sugar fields were often devastated by invasions of the dreaded sugar ant. To protect their sugar crops, French planters used arsenic as a poison. Negro slaves soon learned to use the arsenic to destroy their owners' crops, cattle, wives, children and, of course, their cruel masters as well.

Runaway slaves hid in the countryside and formed ravaging bands which attacked the unwary; they burned, pillaged and raped. Violence on the part of blacks and whites escalated to barbarian intensity.

Jean Berard wrote to his anxious family in New York: "As for our property, I fear we will be unable to control its destiny. We must wait to see what will be spared from destruction."

Streams of Frenchmen poured into New York from Haiti. In the city they joined other French aristocrats and royalty fleeing from their native land, which had been racked by the terror of the French Revolution.

A letter from Monsieur Du Petit-Thouars, a nobleman refugee in America, echoes the terror with which these people lived. Petit-Thouars writes to his sister:

> Great God, with what horror I learned the list of those guillotined. My sisters, my poor sisters! What with yearning in my impatience, I have become almost stupid. I smoke mechanically. I chatter sillily.
>
> O my sister, you are not here to console me, and it is more than a year since you and our other sisters should have known me to be here. I have not received a word from you.

After Jean's worrisome letter arrived, the Berard household awaited his return to New York. Whenever Pierre heard of a ship arriving from Haiti, he would hasten to dockside to make inquiries concerning Monsieur Berard. As each transport arrived bearing Haitian refugees, the political news worsened. One day a ship's captain gave Pierre a letter for Madame Berard. Toussaint rushed home with the note and Madame read it. It was a terse announcement that Jean Berard had died of pleurisy on the plantation.

One night in August, 1797, shortly after Berard's death, when the island was lashed by a tropical storm, bands of slaves swept across its northern portion, burning, looting, and murdering. Hardly a white man, woman or child escaped the awful vengeance. Haiti erupted into a holocaust.

Within two months, well over 1,000 plantations ceased to exist. Clouds of smoke, from which fiery tongues were leaping, hung over the mountains, giving them the appearance of erupting volcanoes.

"The most striking feature of the terrible spectacle," writes an eye-witness named Carteau, "was a rain of fire composed of burning cane straw, which whirled thickly before the blast, like flakes of snow and which the wind carried, now toward the harbor and shipping, now over the houses of the city."

During this time the Berard plantation was wiped out. Although French arms ultimately put down this rebellion, the white man's day in Haiti was over.

*   *   *   *   *

Madame Berard had not yet recovered from the announcement of her husband's death when news arrived of the Berard plantation's destruction. To add to the poor woman's woes, Monsieur Berard's substantial investments in a New York City business were wiped out when the firm collapsed. Madame Berard and her little household were now without resources. Creditors pressed. One day Madame requested Pierre to sell some of her jewelry to pay a long-overdue $40 debt. A few days later the hairdresser returned the jewels.

"Madame, please take these."

"I thought you were to sell those," Marie said.

"It was not necessary, Madame. I had some money left over from my work. Also, I did not spend the generous New Year's present you gave me."

As delicately as possible, Pierre pressed the jewelry on Marie.

"My work is going very well," Pierre explained, "and I would like to arrange to provide a certain sum each week for household expenses until these financial difficulties pass."

French exiles in New York felt it was only a matter of time until French armies and fleets would restore order to Haiti. Madame Berard, nourished by the illusion that her West Indian properties would soon be settled, accepted Pierre's assistance. She planned to repay Toussaint as soon as possible. Like most of her compatriots, Marie Berard badly underestimated black leadership in Haiti. Toussaint L'Ouverture (no relative of Pierre Toussaint), a man of genius and discipline, channeled the volcanic power of the black revolution and welded a superb military force. He secured domination of the island and laid the groundwork for history's first successful slave revolution. After the United States' rebellion against Britain, Haiti's blacks accomplished the Western hemisphere's second successful revolution against a mother country.

L'Ouverture, an intensely practical man, realized that Haiti would need the French planters' expertise if it was to maintain a sound economy. Thus, he invited some planters to return and reclaim their estates. Jean Berard's sisters returned to Haiti to take advantage of L'Ouverture's invitation. Marie Bouquement, a black servant who was Pierre's aunt, returned with the two sisters.

The two women made a fatal mistake. The revolution had utterly destroyed their aristocratic world. Haiti, their beautiful island, lay ravaged, wounded and blasted by the bloodletting, burning, and fighting.

Bryan Edwards, who arrived in northern Haiti in September, 1791, writes:

> We arrived in the harbor of LeCap. . . . The first sight which arrested our attention as we approached was a dreadful scene of devastation by fire. The noble plain adjoining LeCap was covered with ashes, and the surrounding hills, as far as the eye could reach, everywhere presented to us ruins still smoking and houses and plantations at that moment in flames.

The Berard sisters gave Marie Bouquement her freedom and, shortly after, both sisters died. Marie returned to New York City.

*   *   *   *   *

Pierre continued his quiet, tactful support of the Berard household in New York. Sensitive to Madame's need to maintain appearances, he chose to continue as her slave when he had every right to be free. His income was quite substantial; his appointment list grew, and soon he was on call to the wealthiest residents of the city. Among his clients Pierre numbered Mrs. Peter Cruger, granddaughter of General Philip Schuyler, who had defeated the British in the Revolution at Saratoga; Eliza Hamilton, the granddaughter of the ill-fated Alexander; Mrs. Mary Anne Schuyler, the daughter-in-law of General Schuyler; the La Farges, the Livingstons, the Hosacks, and the Binsses. A man of discipline, the hairdresser kept careful accounts of income and expenses. He left no bills unpaid, spent not one penny on himself until all necessities and little luxuries for the Berard household were obtained.

He enjoyed writing letters. The New York Public Library houses five file boxes of Pierre's letters, documents and announcements. The Schuylers had kept them as a family treasure for almost a century. The letters reveal what tradition has maintained—that Toussaint lived for others.

Madame Berard was his first concern, and never in any way did he take advantage of her cruel situation. To outward appearances, Pierre remained a faithful family retainer. Few realized that it was his money that sustained the household.

From his earliest years, Toussaint was a devout man. He began each day by attending six o'clock Mass at St. Peter's Church on Barclay Street. Built in 1785 by a group of 23 Cath-

This mansion, owned by J. C. Stevens, was typical of the homes visited by Pierre. Mrs. Stevens was a great admirer of his.

olics, St. Peter's was New York's first Catholic church. Mass and other prayers finished, Pierre would stop in the city markets. He would always find some little treat for Madame Berard. With this completed, he would return to the Reade Street house for breakfast and begin the day's round of work. Carrying a little bag containing his hairdresser's implements, Pierre made his way on foot from client to client. As a black, he was not allowed to ride the horsecars, but Pierre harbored no resentment. He enjoyed walking, and his lithe, graceful frame and pleasant face cut a joyous figure on the city streets.

An anonymous lady has left us a word picture of Pierre, the hair stylist. She described Toussaint entering the house of a lady of fashion.

> Alice is seated before her glass; a fashionable hairdresser had been sent for, and the illustrious Toussaint, with his good-tempered face, small earrings and white teeth, entered the room, his tall figure arrayed in a spotless apron.
> The curling tongs were heated and there was the perfume of scorched paper as Toussaint commenced operations. Oh, those cruel scissors, they had no mercy upon the beautiful hair. Toussaint's sable face was a most refreshing sight as he went about his work. Soon the elaborate coiffure was completed and Toussaint enchanted with his work. . . .

Toussaint was on his feet 16 hours each day, either working or walking. When he returned he would visit Madame Berard and bring her some little treat, a sweet or confection. Melancholy was gradually enshrouding the once gay Marie. Drawing the curtains of grief about her mind and heart, she was sealing herself off from any pleasurable contact with the outside world.

Pierre tried to cheer her up and some of his happiest moments came when he could set her hair and dress it in the very latest fashion. He overlooked nothing in his fight to drive back the waves of despondency that flowed about poor Madame Berard. He would bring her flowers, encourage her to visit friends, and promote little parties at the Reade Street home. Pierre himself, after his long day's work, would deliver party invitations by hand. The night of the party, Toussaint would set aside his hairdresser's apron, don a red jacket and spotless shirt, and serve as waiter, usher and musician.

Pierre Toussaint

New York's French exiles finally heard good news. A French expeditionary force, supported by Spanish, Dutch, and British elements, had sailed for Haiti. Napoleon had assembled the largest invasion fleet and army that history had ever known and put it under the command of his brilliant young general, Charles Leclerc. War plans called for 20,000 French troops to make the first landing against Toussaint L'Ouverture's ragged black army. Immediately following the initial landings, 20,000 more French troops were to enter combat.

L'Ouverture's black soldiers fought valiantly and quite effectively against this large French force. Both sides sustained enormous casualties. Eventually Toussaint L'Ouverture was betrayed by his own and was delivered into Napoleon's hands. The French then made the fatal mistake of restoring slavery to Haiti. Fighting broke out afresh, but now a new ally joined the blacks. It was yellow fever. The disease struck and struck again. More than 30,000 French soldiers and sailors died. The blacks kept up the military pressure. Eventually the French could fight no longer. Napoleon's armed forces suffered the first defeat

The original St. Peter's, Barclay Street, was the center of the city's rapidly growing Catholic community.

they had ever experienced. The brilliant Leclerc, just 30 years of age, died on Haitian soil, cursing his fate. Fewer than 200 of the original French invaders survived.

The defeat plunged New York's French refugees into new depths of gloom. There was now no hope.

A year after the French debacle in the Caribbean, Monsieur Gabriel Nicolas, a refugee French planter, sought and won Marie Berard's hand. Nicolas, a trained musician, made a fair living playing in New York's theaters. Theatergoing had become more popular and New York boasted a number of new playhouses.

For a time, the new marriage lifted Marie from her despondency. But inevitably the old melancholy returned, and she began to lose interest in daily life more and more. Once again, bad luck dogged Marie. Sobersided religious reformers managed to promote and pass legislation closing many New York theaters. Nicolas' main source of income disappeared. The newly married couple once more found themselves in dire financial straits. And once more Pierre came quickly to the rescue.

Someone once described Pierre Toussaint as God's reflection in ebony. If God is a merciful and kind father, one who loves the afflicted, then certainly Toussaint mirrored him. White and black, in need of money to survive, to keep warm, to purchase freedom from slavery, all found a generous and openhearted friend in Pierre. The black hairdresser not only provided funds but manifested genuine care and concern for the afflicted. Despite his busy schedule and careful husbanding of time, Toussaint was always ready to share the sorrow or burden of another human being. The following appeal is typical of letters found among Toussaint's correspondence:

> My dear Toussaint,
>   It is to you who are the consoler of the unfortunate that I appeal. I beg you, plead with you to come and see me in this place. I have written to some persons, but in vain. Take a carriage. I will pay the fare. God will repay you for this kindness which I ask of you. I have many things to tell you. I beg you, do not fail me. I await you today or tomorrow or even later.
>
> Your unhappy friend,
L. Emmerling
Bellevue Prison

Marie's husband, Gabriel Nicolas, was a musician at the Park Theater, one of New York's most famous.

Toussaint did not manifest mercy without immense personal cost to himself. He was in love with a young black Haitian girl, Juliette Noel. But Toussaint felt that he could not marry Juliette while he bore responsibilities for the Nicolas household.

Marie Nicolas had practically lost her voice and now communicated with Pierre by writing. Madame spent most of her time in her room, her health worsening day by day. Death was not far from her. Marie had one last deed to do before she died.

Summoning Pierre to her room, Madame painfully and slowly whispered to him the news that he was free. An aristocrat to the end, Marie followed the formalities established by the French government. A legal document states:

I, Marie Elisabeth Bossard, wife of Monsieur Gabriel Nicolas, declare with the consent of Mr. Nicolas, my husband, that my intention is that Pierre Toussaint, my slave, shall be and live free of all servitude, and I consent that he enjoy liberty like any other freedman, that this present act be given all the public authenticity it may have. Made at New York, July 2, 1807.

Shortly thereafter, Marie Bossard Nicolas, who had known so much suffering, sorrow and defeat, died. Pierre was with her until the end and summoned a priest before she closed her eyes. He had given his life for her comfort, and now he could rest assured within his own conscience that he had served his mistress well. Few people have experienced such Christian love as Marie Bossard Nicolas.

Now 41 and free of obligations, Toussaint asked Juliette to be his wife. A delightful person, Juliette possessed a joyous spirit and carefree gaiety.

"I would not exchange my Juliette for all the ladies in the world," Pierre exclaimed. "She is beautiful in my eyes."

Juliette and Pierre occupied the third floor of the Reade Street house. Monsieur Nicolas, his cook and the nurse, Marie Bouquement, occupied the first two floors. Pierre continued to serve Monsieur Nicolas in whatever way he could. The Reade Street house became a center of warmth and hospitality. The small apartment was Pierre's credit bureau and employment agency, a shelter for orphans, poor refugee priests and assorted poverty-stricken travelers. Many a French widow or abandoned lady staved off poverty and starvation because Pierre found employment for her, tutoring the children of his wealthy clients.

During the early 19th century, New York public sanitation was primitive. Plagues frequently swept the city, leaving orphans in their wake. Catholics, concerned about the orphans, planned to establish a Catholic orphanage. Pierre, through his clients, both Catholic and Protestant, raised a large amount of money to fund this project. Mother Elizabeth Seton sent three of her Sisters of Charity to begin the work. In August, 1817, the first orphans moved into a little house on Prince Street. Through four decades, Pierre remained a constant support to the orphanage.

Toussaint's concern for plague victims extended beyond mere alms-giving. In those years, yellow fever would strike very often during the month of August in New York. On more than one occasion, Toussaint went fearlessly into the quarantined sections of the city to look for those who might be abandoned in the houses from which people had fled in panic. He was an excellent nurse and was often summoned to watch beside the sick at night. He served the poor, of course, without pay. On one occasion, he found a journeying priest ill with ship fever. He took the priest to his own home and nursed him until his health returned.

One orphan was to have profound influence on Pierre and Juliette's lives. She was Euphemia, the daughter of Pierre's sister, Rosalie, who had died of tuberculosis in 1815. Euphemia could hardly have had a more difficult start in life. Shortly after she was born, her father had abandoned her and her mother.

Euphemia loved to dance and sing and Pierre provided musical training for her. Toussaint himself taught her to read and write in both French and English. At her uncle's orders, Euphemia wrote him each week one letter in French and one in English. It was a difficult and valuable exercise; nearly 500 of Euphemia's letters survive among Toussaint's effects. Nothing escaped the joyous curiosity of the little girl, who was a born reporter. One letter speaks of the first lady balloonist, who soared into the air above Castle Garden and floated eastward across the city. Ungallantly, the balloon dumped the intrepid female into a distant Long

Pierre's wife, Juliette Noel.
He purchased her freedom when she was 15
and she supported his charities.
Juliette was an early patron of
the Oblate Sisters of Baltimore.

Island pond. Euphemia writes: "Did you see the balloon that went up on Thursday afternoon at four o'clock, Uncle? Poor Mrs. Joseph could not see at all. . . . She is in pain with her eyes." Another letter: "I heard that the Italian opera singers have arrived, and you said that when they came, you would go to the theatre. I hope I shall be able to go and see them. . . . I have heard that they cannot speak any other language than Italian." And still another letter: "Have you seen the new Bishop? (Bishop John Dubois) I have not seen him yet. I will go to see him someday at church."

With childish terror she reports what must be one of the earliest predictions of New York's doom. "I heard that an angel appeared to a watchman and told him that the city of New York was to be destroyed by an earthquake on the 15th of the month. Some people say the angel appeared with music, but I do not believe it."

On January 1, 1829, when Euphemia was 14 years old, she wrote to her uncle:

> Dear Uncle:
>
> Will you be pleased to accept my most respectful compliments on the close of the old and the commencement of the new year. Give me leave, dear Uncle, to tell you as well as my poor mind can express itself how truly sensible I am of all your favors. I will try by my conduct to merit the continuance of them.
>
> As it has pleased God to give you good health during the course of the last year, I beseech him to grant you the same to the end of the present and many more. My prayers are morning and night offered up to Heaven for your preservation. Nor are you ever in the day absent from my thoughts.
>
> I remain your dutiful niece,
>
> Euphemia Toussaint

By May the tuberculosis that had plagued Euphemia since infancy claimed her.

Pierre almost broke under the sorrow. When God took her, his faith, so strong, so enduring, so powerful, almost crumbled. Juliette, exhausted by months of nursing Euphemia during this final cruel illness, now had an added burden. She feared for Toussaint's death.

Friends rallied to Pierre and Juliette and did their best to share the burden by their prayers and expressions of sympathy.

Mrs. Cruger, a lifelong friend, wrote as follows: "My heart and soul follow you in your last cares for this cherished child, to whom you have ever been the best, the most tender of fathers. . . . But I could not weep for her, I wept for you. . . ."

Pierre's sense of discipline now sustained him. He kept his hairdressing appointments faithfully, continued to collect for the Catholic orphanage, and manifested his care and concern for all who were in need of his aid or counsel. Although his heart was broken, he refused to withdraw from life. If anything, suffering had deepened him even more. "I go to a great many places," someone recalls Pierre saying; "I go to one house and they cry, cry, cry, cry—somebody dead. I go into another and it is all laughter— they are happy and glad. I go into another and it is all shut up, dark; they move very softly. They speak in a whisper. Somebody very sick. I go to another and it's all dancing, singing, flowers and wedding dresses. I say nothing, but it makes me think a great deal."

*   *   *   *   *

Mary Ann Schuyler, a friend of Pierre's for some 30 years, referred to him as "her saint." The term indicates the good reputation Toussaint enjoyed among his clientele. He could easily have exploited his entree into

Euphemia, adopted daughter of Pierre and Juliette.

the homes of the wealthy to become a fertile source of gossip. Instead, his customers deeply respected and admired Toussaint for his discretion and ability to keep a confidence. To women who would press him for information or gossip, he would simply reply: "Toussaint, Madame, is a hairdresser. He does not gather news."

The widely respected Toussaint did much to lift the clouds of religious and racial prejudice that hung over New York society. As Mrs. Emma Cary, descendant of a famous New York family and convert to Catholicism, writes: "His life was so perfect, and he explained the teaching of the Church with a simplicity so intelligent and courageous that everyone honored him as a Catholic. He would explain the devotion to the Mother of God with the utmost clearness, or show the union of natural and supernatural gifts in the priest. . . . When I was young, I used to hear Protestants speak with reverence of two men—the great Fenelon and the humble Pierre Toussaint!"

Proud to be a black, Toussaint generously assisted his black brothers and sisters in any way he could. Believing education to be a key to a better life, he worked zealously to support the Oblate Sisters of Providence, a religious order of black women established in 1829. Pierre and Juliette were also benefactors of the first New York City Catholic school for black children, St. Vincent de Paul on Canal Street.

Although a member of a black benevolent society, Toussaint refused to be drawn into the slavery debate then raging. Only once, as far as we know, did he ever comment on the

Mrs. Philip (Mary Anne) Schuyler, a New York society woman and a member of a prominent Dutch family in New York. She and her descendants are responsible for much of our knowledge about Pierre.

Pierre provided much of the support for the Prince Street Orphanage,
directed by Mother Seton's Sisters of Charity.

matter. And this, in response to fiery abolitionists who advocated violence
as the means of solving the slavery question: "They have not seen what I have
seen." The Haitian bloodbath memories were still too vivid and painful.

"Toussaint," a lady advised in later years, "you are the richest man
I know. Why not stop working?"

"Then, Madame," he replied, "I should not have enough for others."
In 1851, when Pierre was 85, Juliette died. Toussaint never recovered from
her death. He continued working, but gradually his strength failed. He went
to Mass every morning, but his step grew slower and more uncertain. Spring
came to the city. Toussaint fell ill.

Mrs. George Lee, another lifetime friend, writes to her son of her last visit to Pierre:

> He was feeble, but sitting in an armchair in his dressing gown and supported by pillows. A more perfect representation of a gentleman I have seldom seen. . . . He was overcome when he saw me, and tears fell from his eyes. "It is so changed! So lonely," he said.

Another of his friends, Mrs. Schuyler, asked him, "Pierre, is there anything you want?"

"No," he replied with a serene smile, "nothing on earth." Pierre died June 30, 1853. He was 87.

Toussaint had appointed the Schuyler brothers, George Lee and Robert Lee, as executors of his will. The document was a final expression of his kindness and generosity. Among his final effects, George and Robert found Pierre's last collection for the orphans. It was methodically noted and every penny accounted for.

The brothers removed his metal crucifix from the wall. On the back a hand had written on a little slip of paper: "To Toussaint—from a grateful priest!"

Newspapers carried a full description of his passing and his funeral. The New York *Home Journal* wrote:

> Pierre was respected and beloved by widely different classes of the city. He moved among them in a way peculiarly his own. He possessed a sense of the appropriate, a self respect, and a uniformity of demeanor which amounted to genius.

George Lee Schuyler preserved Toussaint's papers.

The New York *Post* recounted his charities: "Toussaint is spoken of by all who knew him as a man of the warmest and most active benevolence."

Father Quinn, who preached his funeral eulogy, said: "All would be grateful for having known Pierre. . . ; there are few left among the clergy superior to him in zeal and devotion to the Church and for the glory of God; among laymen, not one."

Toussaint was buried alongside Juliette and Euphemia in Old St. Patrick's Cemetery, on Mott Street. As the years passed, his grave was all but forgotten until a young seminarian, now Father Charles McTague, searched out and established the grave site in 1941.

Authorities are presently gathering material with the hope of presenting his cause for beatification.

Revolutionary General Philip Schuyler said it best: "I have known Christians who were not gentlemen, gentlemen who were not Christians. One man I know who is both and that man is black."

An all but obliterated gravestone marks Pierre's burial place in St. Patrick's graveyard on Mott Street.

2. Damien De Veuster

He read the letter over and over. "You may stay as long as your devotion dictates. . . ." The words exploded against his mind and shook his heart. Again, and once again, he read them. They were the most welcome words he had ever received.

He stood and listened to the sounds about him. Soft, cool breezes gently swept across his island. The palm trees along the shore bowed before the refreshing winds, clapping their great fronds. Bright morning sunlight played over the trees, as the Pacific waves rolled tranquilly against the rocky shores. The restless power locked in the Pacific's waves mirrored the surging energies locked within his own heart.

He was a priest—a simple man, this Damien De Veuster. His parents were Belgian farmers. Nature had prepared his square, sturdy and well-developed body to till the soil. God had summoned him to labor in a different field—to cultivate a more violent harvest. The words he now read hammered home this summons.

The letter from his superiors gave Damien permission to stay where he was and where he, in the springtime of 1873, longed with all his heart to

Molokai, the "land of great cliffs," was nearly unapproachable
and an ideal spot on which to isolate lepers.

be—on Molokai, one of the Hawaiian Islands. Father De Veuster, 33, had
already served nine years in the Hawaiian missions. He was a member of the
Fathers of the Sacred Hearts, who had pioneered Catholicism in the islands.

These religious had faced and overcome enormous problems since
their arrival in 1827. Now they faced a new and frightful challenge, a leprosy
epidemic. To halt the spread of the dread disease, the Hawaiian government
had isolated several hundred lepers at Kalawao, on the island of Molokai.
Catholic lepers there begged for a priest. Many missioners, despite danger
of contagion, had offered to go. The Bishop, Louis Maigret, and Father
Modeste, the religious superior of the Sacred Hearts Fathers, had selected
Damien to begin the mission. Both were reluctant to put such a crushing
burden on this young priest's square and sturdy shoulders permanently. The
Bishop and Father Modeste knew the bitter work that had to be done; they

hesitated to demand that this one man do so much of it.

Thirteen years before, while a student for the priesthood in France, Damien had symbolically faced and accepted death. At the public profession of his final vows, as was the religious custom of his times, his superiors covered him with a funeral pall. He had truly believed then that only by accepting death would he discover life. Now he was putting his dedication to the test. He sought to serve the most pitiful of all people, the lepers of Molokai. By so doing, in the words of Robert Louis Stevenson, "he shut too, with his own hands, the doors of his own sepulchre."

* * * * *

The Hawaiian Islands, one of the most beautiful places in all God's creation, were one of the last places on earth that men discovered. God was

A Hawaiian family of the 19th century
sits on a straw mat in front of its grass house.
Their clothes reflect the influence of the Western missionaries.

saving, it seems, his choicest gift for last. Polynesian explorers, the first men to find the islands, settled there about eight centuries after Christ's birth. A thousand years later, during the American Revolution, British sailors, under Captain Cook, were the first Europeans to reach this paradise.

Europeans found about 300,000 people on the islands. The natives—cheerful, unspoiled, and easygoing unless provoked—were generous, and delighted in sports. A highly organized native religion dominated every aspect of Hawaiian life.

Living was easy in the islands. The people readily obtained fish, fruit, vegetables and meat. Hawaiians lived in little homes constructed of palm branches.

As contact with the outside world increased, the Hawaiians, with no immunity to European and Asiatic diseases, suffered immensely. Smallpox, influenza, cholera, tuberculosis, venereal disease struck savagely and pitilessly. Within a hundred years of the white man's arrival, the native population dropped from 300,000 to 50,000 people. In the long litany of ills decimating the Hawaiian people, none was more vicious than leprosy.

One of man's oldest curses, leprosy for centuries defied cure or remedy. To prevent its spread, Moses had separated and isolated Jews afflicted by it from the community. Roman legions and, later, Crusaders brought the disease to Europe. Authorities, having no better remedy than Moses, ordered lepers segregated from the cities and towns. They were

Journalist Walter Gibson
challenged a religious to work
among the lepers.

ordered to wear bells around their necks to warn of their approach. By the year 1000, monks had constructed more than 2000 leper hospitals in Europe. They were called Lazar houses after the Gospel's poor leper, Lazarus.

The first authenticated case of leprosy appeared in Hawaii in 1840. Within 30 years, the disease reached epidemic proportions among the defenseless Hawaiians. Authorities, helpless and ill-equipped, adopted the only policy they knew—segregation. In 1868, the Hawaiian government established a leper settlement on the island of Molokai, and officials were dispatched to round up the lepers.

Ideally equipped by nature for its grim purposes, Molokai became an island of sorrow in the wild beauty of the Hawaiian chain. Its very name struck terror in the Hawaiian heart.

*　　*　　*　　*　　*

Her name was Karokina. Mother of three children, she lived in a tiny fishing village on the island of Hawaii. Her life was simple, serene; her home, a lean-to built of palm branches. Affection, laughter and song characterized Karokina's home life. She loved to watch the sun cast down silver jewels of light upon the green ocean. The gods were close to Karo. Every so often, Pele, goddess of fire, whose footsteps the medicine men declared had formed their islands, hurled smoke and fire from a nearby volcano. Then Karo knew fear. The blue skies turned to black, the ocean hissed as hot lava and firestones poured into its bosom. Then sun and moon hid their

At 33 Fr. Damien DeVeuster
accepted the challenge.

Damien was a skilled carpenter. With the help of the lepers he added a wing to the chapel and built a rectory.

faces behind the great clouds of steam that rose from the heaving seas.

Then the winds cleared the air, and Karo's fear passed. Karo loved her islands most in the spring, when the poinciana trees burst into masses of scarlet, orange and gold blossoms, and pink flowers popped out from the green canopies of the monkeypod trees. It was during a springtime of great joy and beauty that white men from Honolulu came to Karo's village. They were searching for natives who had leprosy.

Karo had the illness. She knew a few years before, when her hand brushed against a smoldering log, and she felt no pain. The terrible illness had begun its frightful work. Her face's gentle features gradually withered. Her eyes narrowed and her ears enlarged. The disease ate her energy, and she knew fever and weakness. Karo's husband and children sorrowed at her plight and did all they could to comfort her. They, of course, kept her at home. Her husband heard that the government was rounding up lepers and sending them to Molokai. "How cruel," he complained to his neighbors, "to separate mother or father or children from home when they need the family most. If the white man wishes to treat his sick differently than Hawaiians do, why doesn't he go away and leave us alone? He forced his cruel illness on us and now he is forcing his brutal cures."

There were other lepers in Karo's village. Some heard the white men coming and hid in the great volcano caves. Others found hiding places and holes in the jungle floor. But for Karo it was too late. The hunters took her at gunpoint to a government schooner. Her husband tried to stop them, but was helpless. Karo's children wailed and wept tears of despair. White men spoke of their god as a god of mercy. Yet they showed no mercy.

Karo's captors took her first to Honolulu, where they herded her together with lepers from other islands. Some were more disfigured and ill than she was. Many could not walk; others could barely crawl. But the police forced them all on board the ship that was to take them to Molokai in this February of 1873. The ship's captain and crew looked on the unfortunates with horror.

After several hours on the open sea, the schooner, full of weeping and terrorized sick, arrived off the Molokai colony's shore. There was no harbor, no dock. The captain and crew, afraid to bring the vessel too close to the rocky beach, drove and hurled the lepers into the surf. Some drowned. Others miraculously survived. On torn and bleeding feet they stumbled up on the harsh volcanic rock, numb with cold.

There was no one to greet them. No one to warm them. Many survived the pounding surf only to die from exhaustion on the inhospitable beach.

Karo dragged herself to shore. Eventually she found a little cave to shelter her shivering body. Wild fruit helped nourish her. There was little food. She soon joined another group of lepers. They told her to forget home. All of them were condemned. They might as well reach for whatever wild joys they could possess before merciful death claimed them.

"In this place," a man advised Karo, "there is no law." Sexual immorality, brawling, drunkenness, robberies, and orgiastic dancing, fueled by a narcotic made from tree roots, characterized the lives of many lepers. Nobody cared. When lepers died, their poor bodies were thrown into graves so shallow that pigs and dogs grew fat feasting on their flesh.

Karo despaired and died.

Between 1866 and 1873, 797 lepers arrived at Molokai. Almost half died. Public indignation mounted. The Board of Health, which natives wryly dubbed the "Board of Death," sought to improve conditions. The government granted an increase in leper food and clothing rations, and appointed a superintendent to restore law and order to the colony. The press kept up a drumfire of complaints about the ill-treatment and disorder of Molokai. In April, 1873, Walter Gibson, a colorful and clever politician, wrote in Nuhou, a Hawaiian newspaper:

> If a noble Christian priest, preacher or sister should be inspired to go and sacrifice a life to console these poor wretches, that would be a royal soul to shine forever on a throne reared by human love.

Despite the fulsome prose, Gibson was trumpeting a challenge. There were indeed several men in the islands only too willing to respond. They were priests and Brothers of the Sacred Hearts. One of them was Father Damien De Veuster. Call it presentiment or prophecy, but Damien had known for some time that he would eventually go to Molokai. In April, 1873, he wrote his Father General in Europe about his mission in Kohala, Hawaii, where he was stationed. "Many of our Christians here at Kohala also had to go to Molokai. I can only attribute to God an undeniable feeling that soon I shall join them. . . . Eight years of service among Christians you love and who love you have tied us by powerful bonds." And join them he did. In early May, 1873, Father Damien's superiors approved this request to serve at the leper settlement.

Bishop Maigret accompanied Damien to Molokai. The Bishop proudly presented the new pastor to the Catholic lepers. The joy of their welcome and Damien's excitement upon finally arriving at Molokai dimmed the fact that he carried with him little more than his breviary. Sacred Hearts religious previously had built a tiny chapel on Molokai, and had dedicated it to St. Philomena. For his first rectory, Damien used the shelter of a pandanus tree, beside the little church. The pandanus offered hospitality to all passing creatures—centipedes, scorpions, ants, roaches and, finally, fleas. Cats, dogs and sheep found shelter under the tree's kind branches. Damien settled in comfortably. A large rock on the side of the tree served as his dinner table. During these first weeks the new missionary took normal precautions to avoid contagion.

But if Damien protected his body, there was nothing he could do to protect his eyes or ears or sense of smell from the shock of contact with the leper. Here at Kalawao, the priest had opened a door to hell. Victims of the disease were all about him, their bodies in ruins, their faces ravaged and smashed by the voracious bacillus. The constant coughing of the sick was the colony's most familiar sound. Gathering up his enormous resources of courage, Damien began to approach the lepers one by one. Their breath was fetid; ·their bodies, already in a state of corruption, exuded a most foul odor. One of his first visits was to a young girl. He found that worms had eaten her whole side.

"Many a time," he wrote as he recalled these first days, "in fulfilling my priestly duties at the lepers' homes, I have been obliged, not only to close my nostrils, but to remain outside to breathe fresh air. To counteract the bad smell, I got myself accustomed to the use of tobacco. The smell of the pipe preserved me somewhat from carrying in my clothes the obnoxious odor of our lepers."

Molokai's first lepers lived on, died on and were buried in their mats. Though weakened by the disease, they were expected to till the soil and raise cattle in order to feed themselves.

Molokai was a colony of shame, peopled by lost souls and smashed bodies. Medical care was minimal. Even if decent care was provided, Hawaiians distrusted the white man's medicine, preferring their own witch doctors or "kahuna." White doctors sporadically appeared at government expense. These physicians lived in terror of contagion. One doctor examined lepers' wounds by lifting their bandages with his cane. Another left medicine on a table where lepers could collect it without touching him.

Life was grotesque. Ambrose Hutchinson, a veteran of half a century in the colony, describes an incident in the settlement's early days.

> A man, his face partly covered below the eyes, with a white rag or handkerchief tied behind his head, came out from the house that stood near the road. He was pushing a wheelbarrow loaded with a bundle, which, at first, I mistook for soiled rags. He wheeled it across the yard to a small windowless shack. . . . The man then half turned over the wheelbarrow and shook it. The bundle (instead of rags, it was a human being) rolled out on the floor with an agonized groan. The fellow turned the wheelbarrow around and wheeled it away, leaving the sick man lying there helpless. After a while the dying man raised and pushed himself in the doorway; with his body in and his legs stretched out, he lay there face down.

Molokai was a chamber of horrors. But the Hawaiian government (which at this time was independent of the United States and headed by native royalty) had not planned it that way.

The Board of Health had put much thought into the leper settlement's establishment. It chose Molokai because its geography was ideal for enforcing the isolation and segregation policy. Like other Hawaiian islands, Molokai was formed by a volcanic eruption from the ocean floor. As the fires under the crust of the earth exploded upward, Molokai rose out of the sea, a spectacular palisade reaching three to four thousand feet above the ocean. A later eruption within the high island poured hot lava into the sea. The volcanic flow piled up until it formed a shelf at the base of Molokai's high cliffs. This peninsula sticks out into the ocean like a dirty brown furrowed tongue. There is no way to leave the peninsula except to plunge into the ocean or to climb up the huge vertical precipice surrounding the peninsula on three sides. The Board of Health knew that the peninsula was a natural prison, for no one suffering the ravages of leprosy could possibly scale the cliffs surrounding the colony. Most of Molokai's nonleper population lived on the high plateau which embraces more than 90 percent of the island's land area. The leper colony was established at Kalawao on a part of the peninsula described above.

Molokai's palisades are covered with heavy green vegetation. Great cataracts of water from the frequent rainstorms that lash Molokai plunge down her cliffsides. At certain seasons of the year, winds carrying chill and dampness cascade down from the mountains onto the leper colony. Huddled in their flimsy huts, the lepers suffered grievously from the cold. "A heavy windstorm," Damien reported after arrival, "blew down most of the rotten abodes, and many a weakened leper lay in the wind and rain with his blanket and wet clothing."

*   *   *   *   *

At the outset of his mission Damien aimed to restore in each leper a sense of personal worth and dignity. To show his poor battered flock the value of their lives, he had to demonstrate to them the value of their deaths. And so he turned his attention first to the cemetery area beside the little chapel. He fenced it around to protect the graves from the pigs, dogs, and other scavengers. He constructed coffins and dug graves. He organized the lepers into the Christian Burial Association to provide decent burial for the dead. The organization arranged for the requiem Mass, the proper funeral ceremonies, and sponsored a musical group that played during the funeral procession.

Damien continued to minister to the sick, bringing the sacraments of confession and Holy Communion and anointing. He washed their bodies, bandaged their wounds and tidied their rooms and beds. He did all he could to make them as comfortable as possible.

He encouraged lepers to help him in all his activities. With their assistance, he built everything from coffins to cottages. He constructed the rectory, built a home for the lepers' children. When the colony expanded

Deeply moved by the plight of leper children, Damien struggled to preserve them from the physical and moral corruption of Molokai.

along the peninsula to Kalaupapa, he hustled the lepers into construction of a good road between Kalawao and Kalaupapa. Under his direction, lepers blasted rocks at the Kalaupapa shoreline and opened a decent docking facility. Damien taught his people to farm, to raise animals, to play musical instruments, to sing. He watched with pride as the leper bands he organized marched up and down playing the music Hawaiians love so much. No self-pity in this colony. Damien's cheerful disposition and desire to serve touched the lepers' hearts without patronizing or bullying them. Little by little their accomplishments restored the sense of dignity that their illness threatened to destroy.

Damien was everywhere on the island. Although the administration of the colony was under the government, Damien's impetuosity prevented his observing jurisdictional lines. If there was need and he could help, he would do so.

He harried government authorities. In their eyes he was "obstinate, headstrong, brusk and officious." Joseph Dutton, who came to help on Molokai, later on speaks of him as

> . . . vehement and excitable in regard to matters that did not seem to him right, and he sometimes said and did things that he afterwards regretted . . . , but he had a true desire to do right, to bring about what he thought was best. No doubt he erred sometimes in judgment. . . . In certain periods, he got along smoothly with everyone, and at all times, he was urgent for improvements. In some cases, he made for confusion, as various government authorities would not agree with him.

In all things his lepers came first. It would be a mistake, however, to think of Damien as a single-minded fanatic. He was a human being who was quick to smile, of pleasant disposition, of open and frank countenance.

No one could deny that he was a headstrong person. But no one who knew him could deny that he was a man of warm and tender heart. He quickly forgave injuries and never bore a grudge.

Charles Warren Stoddard, an American writer, first visited Molokai in 1868, five years before Damien's arrival. He returned in 1884. In place of the miserable huts of the colony's beginning, Stoddard now found two villages of white houses, surrounded by flower gardens and cultivated fields. Molokai boasted a decent hospital, a graveyard, and two orphanages filled with children. But what delighted Stoddard most of all was that the men and women, instead of rotting in the slime, awaiting death, were out horseback-riding.

In 1888, the Englishman Edward Clifford visited Damien. "I had gone to Molokai expecting to find it scarcely less dreadful than hell itself," Clifford wrote, "and the cheerful people, the lovely landscapes, and comparatively painless life were all surprises. These poor people seemed singularly happy."

Clifford asked lepers if they missed not being back home. They replied, "Oh, no! We're well off here. The government watches over us, the superintendent is good, and we like our pastor. He builds our houses himself, he gives us tea, biscuits, sugar and clothes. He takes good care of us and doesn't let us want for anything."

*   *   *   *   *

Damien was completely aware of the Hawaiian's childlike nature. Simple, generous, hospitable people, the Hawaiians were most attractive. They remained, however, children of Adam and could be licentious, lazy, and, at times, mean-spirited. Damien was not blind to their defects. Ambrose Hutchinson describes the immorality that continued to plague the colony despite Damien's best efforts.

Drinkers and dancers met in a remote area of the leper settlement called "the crazy pen." From time to time Damien raided this scabrous spot, and with his walking stick he broke up the dancing and knocked over the liquor bottles. Hutchinson wrote that, "The hilarious feasters made a quick getaway from the place through the back door to escape Damien's big stick. He would not hesitate to lay it on good and hard on the poor hapless one who happened to come within reach of his cane."

His disciplinary measures did not hurt church attendance. The lepers came to St. Philomena's in such numbers that he had to enlarge the chapel. But even expanded facilities could not contain the worshipers. On Sundays, overflow crowds peered through the church windows.

Visitors never forgot the sights and sounds of a Sunday Mass at St. Philomena's Chapel. Damien, clear-eyed and devout, stood at the altar. Strong, muscular, a picture of vitality and health, the priest's face was kind and his concern for the people was evident. His lepers gathered about him at the altar. Some were blind. They constantly coughed and expectorated. The odor was overpowering. Yet Damien never once wavered or showed his disgust. Damien placed, of all things, poor boxes in the church. Because the blind often missed the slot, the pastor placed a little bell inside the poor box. When the sightless leper's coin had dropped safely into the box, the bell rang.

Hawaiians love to sing, and St. Philomena's choir had no shortage of candidates. Because leprosy often attacked vocal cords, leper voices produced peculiar sounds. Nevertheless, the choir sang joyfully.

Damien's life was suffused with horror, yet he refused to be swept into despair. He ran footraces for the sports-loving lepers, even though some of them had no feet. He formed a band, even though some had few fingers to play the instruments. One witness reported two organists who played at the same time, managing ten fingers between them.

*   *   *   *   *

News of Damien's deeds spread from Hawaii to Europe to America. The priest of Molokai became front-page news. Funds poured in from all over the world. An Anglican priest, Reverend Hugh Chapman, organized, through the help of *The London Times,* a highly successful fund drive.

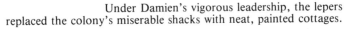

Under Damien's vigorous leadership, the lepers replaced the colony's miserable shacks with neat, painted cottages.

But Damien's notoriety and fund-raising drew the ire of the Hawaiian government and his own religious superiors. Both accused him of playing to the press for his own selfish reasons. The government was unhappy, because it felt Damien's begging played down the Hawaiian effort to combat leprosy. Walter Gibson, Prime Minister of the Hawaiian king, felt that his government was most generous toward the lepers. It was spending $50,000 a year, which represented five percent of its total taxes, on leper care. No other government in the world could point to such a proud health-care record.

The superiors of the Sacred Hearts mission were distressed because they felt Damien was giving the congregation's Fathers and Brothers a bad image. The press made it seem as if he were the only Sacred Hearts missionary willing to serve the colony. His superiors knew this was not true. And they took it as an affront to the whole congregation. His superiors further accused Damien of being a "loner" because of his unhappy relationship with the three assistants they had sent him at different times. In all fairness, it probably is true that no one else could have lived with any of the three priests. But no one was more irritated by Damien's fame than Hawaii's Yankee missionaries.

Stern puritan divines felt that leprosy was the inevitable result of the Hawaiian people's licentiousness. In their puritanical judgment the Hawaiian people were corrupt and debased. The segregation policy would have to be enforced to hasten the inevitable physical and moral collapse of the essentially rotten Hawaiian culture. There were medical doctors who were so convinced of an essential connection between leprosy and sexual immorality that they insisted that leprosy could be spread only through sexual contact.

When Damien entered his prison at Molokai, he had to make a decision. He believed that the Hawaiians were basically good and not essentially corrupt. And now he had to show them his belief, regardless of the price. Thus, somewhere during the first part of his stay he made the dread decision to set aside his fears of contagion. He touched the lepers, he embraced them, he dined with them, he cleaned and bandaged their wounds and sores. He placed the Host upon their battered mouths. He put his thumb on their foreheads when he anointed them with the holy oil. All these actions involved touch. Touch is, of course, necessary if one is to communicate love and concern. The Hawaiians understood this. And that is why the Hawaiians shrank from the Yankee divines. They sensed the contempt in which the puritan minds held them.

Damien was not, as we have noted, blind to the Hawaiians' very real faults. Many Hawaiians, by their irregular sex habits, greatly contributed to the spread of leprosy. But Damien knew that was not the only way the disease was communicated. Above all, he rejected the insufferable notion that God had laid this disease as a curse upon these people, to wipe them off the face of the earth. Damien hated leprosy. He didn't see it as a tool of a vengeful God. He saw it as a suffering that man must eliminate. God loved the leper. No man had the right to scorn him.

Thus, very early in his apostolate at Molokai, Damien was impelled to identify himself as closely as possible with his lepers. Long before he had the disease, he spoke of himself and the people of Molokai as "we lepers." Six months after his arrival at Kalawao he wrote his brother in Europe, ". . . I make myself a leper with the lepers to gain all to Christ. That is why, in preaching, I say 'we lepers'; not, 'my brethren. . . . ' "

Damien embraced the leper but not leprosy. He lived in great dread of the disease. When he first experienced leprosy's symptomatic itching, while still a missionary at Kohala, some years before he went to Molokai, he knew then that the loathsome disease threatened him. Even when the disease had run a good bit of its brutal course through his body, he still at times seemed to refuse to admit that he was a victim. But leprosy finally claimed him. It was the final price God exacted from Damien to show his sense of community and oneness with his poor afflicted flock.

Some said there was a connection between leprosy and venereal disease. In order to witness against those who claimed leprosy could only be spread by sexual contact, Damien submitted to the indignity of having his blood and body examined in detail after he had contracted the disease. Doctor Arning, a world-famous specialist in the disease, reported after examination, that Damien had no sign of syphilis. In a signed statement dictated to Brother Joseph Dutton, his co-worker, Damien wrote, "I have never had sexual intercourse with anyone whomsoever."

History has borne out the wisdom of Damien's decision to take these embarrassing measures. Shortly after Damien's death, a Yankee divine of Honolulu, Doctor Charles McEwen Hyde, bitterly attacked the priest's moral life. The good clergyman claimed that Damien got leprosy because he was licentious.

Father Damien was not lacking defenders. In a magnificent statement, Robert Louis Stevenson, who had visited Molokai after Damien's death, rose to champion the priest's cause. The author's defense of Damien rested upon the complete sacrifice the man made of his life. A sacrifice no Yankee missionary in Hawaii had duplicated.

If some white missionaries scorned Father Damien, most Hawaiians loved him. In September, 1881, Hawaiian Princess Liliuokalani visited Molokai. The Princess, moved deeply by the lepers' suffering, was unable to give the speech she had prepared. Leaving Molokai with a broken heart, she returned to Honolulu and requested Father Damien to accept the Hawaiian Order of Knight Commander of the Royal Order of Kalakaua in recognition of his "efforts in alleviating the distress and mitigating the sorrows of the unfortunate." With pleasure, Damien accepted the award. He felt that it would bring attention to his lepers. There were many Americans, too, both in Hawaii and on the mainland, who recognized the work that Damien was doing and who sent, with characteristic American generosity, funds and other forms of help to him. In Honolulu, American Protestants

Charles McEwen Hyde—he bitterly attacked the priest's moral life.

were among his most generous benefactors. Opening their hearts and their purses to Damien, they sent him food, medicines, clothing, and all sorts of help for his mission.

*   *   *   *   *

Damien was alone on the frontier of death. His loneliness oppressed him. He speaks of his "black thoughts" and the "insupportable melancholy that arose from his lack of religious companionship." The Board of Health remonstrated with him because, ignoring the isolation policy, he climbed up and down the palisades to build chapels and to bring the sacraments to the healthy people who dwelt on Molokai's plateau. His superiors were displeased with his trips to Honolulu. They felt he gave bad example in the face of the government's policy on segregation of the lepers. Furthermore, two Sacred Hearts Fathers, laboring in other parts of the Hawaiian Islands, had contracted leprosy. The superiors did not want to force them to Molokai. They felt that Damien, by leaving the colony, might just precipitate a government crackdown.

He continually begged his superiors for a confrere, not only to assist him in the ever-mounting work, but also to provide spiritual comfort for him. He hungered above all, for a priestly companion to whom he could confess and receive the sacrament of Penance. His writing reveal his concern that he would forget the true pur-

Author Robert Louis Stevenson championed the priest's cause.

pose of his life. In a little notebook, he counseled himself:

> Be severe toward yourself, indulgent toward others. Have scrupulous exactitude regarding God: prayer, meditation, Mass, administration of the Sacraments. Unite your heart with God. . . . Remember always your three vows, by which you are dead to the things of the world. Remember always that God is eternal, and work courageously in order one day to be united with him forever.

During one time when the isolation policy was being strictly enforced, a ship's captain, reacting to the government's orders, forbade Damien's bishop to disembark on Molokai. In order to see the bishop, Damien sailed out to the boat. The captain refused Damien's request to board. The priest pleaded in vain with the captain, saying that he wanted to confess his sins. "Bishop," the priest called to the boat, "will you hear my confession from here?" The bishop consented, and Damien, in an exercise of humility that touched all who witnessed it, confessed his sins aloud to the bishop.

One day in December, 1884, while soaking his feet in extremely hot water, Father De Veuster experienced no sensation of heat or pain. The evil disease he had confronted for so long now claimed him. In his last years, he engaged in a flurry of activity. He hastened to complete his many build-

"The Lord decorated me with his own particular cross—leprosy."

Through the generosity of Henry P. Baldwin, Damien established
a home for leper boys.

ing projects, enlarge his orphanages, organize his work.

Help came to him from four unexpected sources. A priest, a soldier, a male nurse, and a nun. The soldier, Joseph Dutton, was a most unusual man. He had survived Civil War combat, a broken marriage, several years of hard drinking, to show up on Molokai's shores in July, 1886. He stayed 45 years without ever leaving the colony. He served the lepers of the Baldwin Home for Boys. Joseph was never seriously ill until just before his death in 1931, just short of 88.

Another layman, James Sinnett, a man who had a colorful and checkered career, during which he gained some experience in nursing in Mercy Hospital, Chicago, came to Molokai eight months before Father Damien died. The leper priest called him "Brother James." He nursed Father Damien during the final phase of his illness, and closed his eyes in

Women and girls who were members of the leper colony.

death. During the last days of Damien's life, Sinnett served as his secretary. He was faithful to the very end, and when Damien died, Sinnett left the colony. Nothing was heard from him thereafter.

Father Louis-Lambert Conrardy, a fellow Belgian, joined Father Damien May 17, 1888. Archbishop William Gross of Oregon generously permitted Father Conrardy to leave his own priest-poor area to labor in Molokai. Archbishop Gross wrote of Conrardy, "I have tramped all over Oregon with Father Conrardy and he is a noble, heroic man. . . . Though he knows and realizes perfectly that he might succumb to the disease, his voluntary going is real heroism." Conrardy and Damien provided the spiritual and social companionship that Damien so desperately craved.

The sister who now offered support for Damien and his work at this critical junction was Mother Marianne Kopp, superior of the Franciscan Sisters of Syracuse, New York, who served the Honolulu leper hospital.

Damien requested Mother Marianne to send sisters to care for the girls' orphanage at Molokai. Mother Marianne, calming the fears of one of the sisters who was afraid she would contract leprosy, gently counseled her, "Do not allow it (the fear of leprosy) to trouble you, and when the thought comes to you, drive it from your mind, and remember, you will never be a leper; nor will any Sister of our Order." The Franciscan Sisters of Syracuse are still at Molokai. To this day, not one of them has ever contracted leprosy.

In 1886 Father Damien wrote to his superior:

> As I wrote to you about two years ago that I had then suspicions of the first germs of leprosy being in my system—the natural consequence of a long stay with these lepers—be not surprised or too much pained to know that one of your spiritual children is decorated not only with the Royal Cross of King Kalakaua, but also with the cross more heavy, and considered less honorable, of leprosy with which our Divine Savior has permitted me to be stigmatized.

The announcement that Damien had leprosy hit his own religious superiors, Father Fouesnel and his bishop, Hermann Koeckemann, like a thunderbolt. Damien was the third Sacred Hearts missionary stricken with leprosy. To prevent further infection, Father Fouesnel forbade Damien to

A small boat makes its way through the pounding surf at Molokai.

visit the mission headquarters of the Sacred Hearts Fathers in Honolulu. "If you come," Father Superior advised Damien, "you will be relegated to a room which you are not to leave until your departure."

Father Fouesnel suggested that if Damien insisted on coming to Honolulu, he stay at the Franciscan Sisters' leper hospital. "But if you go there," the superior counseled, "please do not say Mass. For neither Father Clement nor I will consent to celebrate Mass with the same chalice and the same vestments you have used. The Sisters will refuse to receive Holy Communion from your hands." One can understand the superior's concern. But Damien was being forced, nevertheless, to consume the bitter wine of loneliness to its dregs. He now knew not only the physical sufferings of Christ but the harrowing loneliness and abandonment of the Savior. Damien did

go to Honolulu and remained at the leprosarium from July 10 to 16. It was during the time that he arranged with Mother Marianne to come to Molokai. He spoke of his rejection by his own as "the greatest suffering he had ever endured in his life."

Doctor Mouritz, medical attendant at Molokai, charted the progress of the physical dissolution of Damien's body. He writes: "The skin of the abdomen, chest, the back, is beginning to show tubercles, masses of infiltration. . . . The membranes of the nose, roof of the mouth, pharynx, and larynx are involved; the skin of his cheeks, nose, lips, forehead, and chin is excessively swollen. . . . His body is becoming emaciated."

Joseph Dutton, a Civil War veteran, assisted Damien.

An ever-deepening mental distress accompanied Damien's physical dissolution. A severe depression, as well as religious scruples, now plagued the leper priest. Damien felt he was unworthy of heaven. The rejection by his religious superiors left him in near disarray. Once he claimed: "From the rest of the world I received gold and frankincense, but from my own superiors myrrh" (a bitter herb).

As death approached, Father Damien engaged in a flurry of activity. He worked as much as his wounded and broken body would permit him. He wrote his bishop, entreating not to be dispensed from the obligation of the breviary, which he continued to recite as best he could as his eyes failed. The disease invading his windpipe progressed to such an extent that it kept him from sleeping more than an hour or two at night. His voice was reduced to a raucous whisper. Leprosy was in his throat, his lungs, his stomach, and his intestines. After ravaging his body outwardly, it was now destroying him from within.

As the end drew near, priests of his own congregation came to hear his confession. The leper priest had requested a funeral pall, which the Franciscan Sisters made for him and delivered from Honolulu. It arrived the same day. Two more weeks of suffering, and on April 15, 1889, Damien died. It was Holy Week. Some weeks before, Damien had said that the Lord wanted him to spend Easter in heaven.

Once he had written, "The cemetery, the church and rectory form one enclosure; thus at nighttime I am still keeper of this garden of the dead,

Sister Marianne from Syracuse, N. Y., brought nursing nuns to the colony.

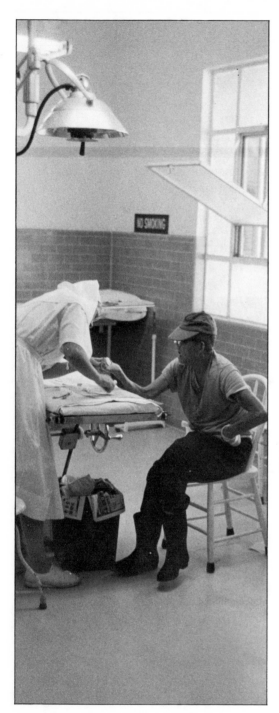

where my spiritual children lie at rest. My greatest pleasure is to go there to say my beads and meditate on that unending happiness which so many of them are already enjoying." And now it was his turn to occupy a little plot of ground in "his garden of the dead."

He no longer meditated on that unending happiness, but now most surely possessed it. Long ago he had selected the precise spot for his grave amid the 2000 lepers buried in Molo-kai cemetery. Coffin bearers laid him to rest under his pandanus tree. It was the same tree that had sheltered him the day he read those fateful words: "You may stay as long as your devotion dictates. . . ."

Franciscan sisters still tend
the colony's dwindling population today.

3. Frederic Ozanam

Paris was burning. The French themselves had set it on fire. Great piles of gray, yellow and black smoke poured from some of the city's magnificent buildings, bearing on their filthy billows, the harsh odors of burning walls, furniture, draperies and paint. These fumes, acrid as they were, could not conceal the stench of death that hung over the tortured city. Hundreds of corpses littered the narrow, twisting streets and broad boulevards of the city. Cries of the wounded fused with shouts of hatred to create a wild and merciless melody that soared above the thumps of mortars, the whine of rifle fire, and the pounding of artillery.

It was June, 1848. The French had locked themselves into that most vicious of conflicts, civil war. Crying "bread or death," France's desperate poor had risen against their government. Federal authorities, long alert for a revolution, sent 40,000 Army National Guard and police to crush the uprising. And now, during this third day of furious fighting, Paris had gone mad with its own blood.

In one sector of the city, a National Guard patrol, inching its way through a winding street, suddenly came under rebel fire. The insurgents, firing from behind barricades they had constructed from cobblestones torn out of the streets, quickly pinned down the patrol. The guardsmen hunkered behind a garden wall, seeking shelter from the hail of bullets. One of the patrol, Frederic Ozanam, 35, a university professor in ordinary life, felt the barrel of his rifle. It was cold. This was Ozanam's third day in combat and he had not yet fired the weapon. He hoped and prayed he would not have to shoot.

Guardsman Ozanam was no coward. His reluctance to shoot arose, not from fear, but from love. Frederic knew the people he was fighting much better than the cruel and ambitious politicians who led this ruinous revolt. He could hear some of them now, cursing and swearing from behind their stone fortress, challenging the patrol to charge. These were not the rebels' true voices. Theirs was the voice of the poor. He had listened to them and loved them for years. It was only a matter of time, Frederic knew, until the government forces crushed these brave, courageous people. For Ozanam these few days were a nightmare. He was torn between two duties: to defend his nation and to protect his poor.

Cruel dilemmas were not new to Frederic Ozanam. Indeed, it seemed that he was born to endure them.

Frederic's father, Jean Antoine Francois Ozanam, was a brave man. He had the honors to prove it. As a young cavalry officer in Napoleon's army, he had been decorated for conspicuous gallantry by Napoleon himself. Retired from the army at age 25, Jean later studied medicine and became a doctor in Italy. During a typhus epidemic in 1813, the new doctor served so courageously that the Italian government granted him the Iron Crown, an award of highest degree.

In that same plague year, the doctor's wife, the former Marie Nantes, surprised Jean with their fifth child, a boy, whom they christened Frederic. The surprise was not so much that Marie had a child—she was to have no less than 14—but that this baby survived. Only three Ozanam children would reach adulthood.

Two years following Frederic's birth the Ozanams returned to Lyons, France, their native city.

As Frederic grew into his teens, he manifested an unusual degree of intelligence, a gentle sense of humor, and a winning personality. The Ozanam offspring could also be stubborn, heedless and, like most teenagers, lazy.

Frederic read much of the anti-Catholic literature so popular in France during these years. His young mind, though sharp, was incapable of wrestling with intellectual giants who strode across the French landscape, casting thunderbolts of scorn, ridicule and hatred for religion. Soon, young Frederic, over his head in his reading, was drowning in doubt.

The troubled teenager studied as many Catholic books as he could. They did not help. He prayed for rescue; his prayers went unanswered. One day, kneeling before the Blessed Sacrament, Frederic promised the Lord to spend his life defending the Catholic religion. "But," he prayed, "how can I defend what I do not have? Only you, Lord, can restore my faith to me."

A short time later, Father Noirot, a teacher at the Lyons college

The poor paid the highest price in blood,
suffering and starvation during the period of the 1848 revolution.

Frederic attended, took the young doubting Thomas under his wing. Convinced that Frederic needed fresh air as much as spiritual counseling, the priest and his youthful disciple strolled day after day through the verdant woodland on the islands and riverbanks surrounding Lyons, probing the great problems of faith. Noirot literally walked off the young man's season of doubt. Frederic's doubts slowly disappeared, his depression lifted, and his normal good spirits returned. This painful passage behind him, young Ozanam now turned to face a fresh trial.

Doctor Ozanam dreamed a great dream for his son. Frederic, so obviously gifted, would pursue a successful law career, make a good living, and be a consolation to the doctor and his wife in their old age. The doctor's dream was not unrealistic. Only one obstacle prevented its coming true.

Frederic hated law; he yearned instead to dedicate his life to literary studies. The usually compassionate and understanding father stubbornly insisted Frederic become an attorney. Feeling duty-bound to obey, Frederic left Lyons in his 19th year to undertake law courses at Paris' famous University of the Sorbonne.

A short time after his arrival at the university in late fall, 1831, Frederic, homesick, lonely and, no doubt, feeling full of self-pity for yielding to his father's wishes, wrote home: "I hate Paris, I am chained to it as to a corpse. Its cold congeals my blood . . . its corruption paralyzes my spirit. . . ."

A sketch by a friend
shows Ozanam as a young man.
As he stood on the threshold of manhood,
filled with a sense of mission, he was
determined to bring Christ to the world.

Frederic Ozanam

If Doctor Ozanam experienced little joy as he read those words, he must have felt almost completely depressed when his son later wrote, "In Paris I am buried and lost."

But Doctor Ozanam correctly judged that his son would not stay isolated for long. The irrepressible Frederic, with his warm and cheerful personality, inevitably attracted friends.

At first, law studies left little time for social life. Ozanam recalls in later years, "Many a time, in those first days, the shaded light of my lamp and the glowing embers of the fire were my only companions from tea to bed."

But within a few months Frederic had many student chums and became so involved in university life that he gave less time to sleep and less concentration to his studies. His natural energy made up for his lack of sleep; his extraordinary intelligence, for fewer study hours.

It was the unhappy lot of Catholics at the university that first drew Frederic into student affairs. Certain Sorbonne faculty members made it a practice to distort and mock Catholic teachings. Catholic students sat silent and helpless during these lectures, fearing these teachers would fail them or

As a troubled teenager, Frederick would often walk this path on the Isle of Barbe, with the gentle and learned Father Noirot.

expel them if they objected. Young Ozanam, a born leader, appealed to all Sorbonne students' sense of fair play, and mounted petitions demanding the opportunity to reply to the charges against the faith. So effectively did Frederic rally the students' assistance that he could gleefully write home, "Every time a professor raises his voice against our faith, Catholic voices are now raised in protest." The mocking soon stopped.

In another effort to revitalize the Sorbonne's dispirited Catholics, Frederic joined a revered professor, Monsieur Bailly de Surcy, in reviving a defunct Catholic discussion club. This venture was to have an outcome that neither Bailly nor Ozanam, in their wildest imaginings, could foresee. The club, encouraging free discussions, attracted professors, scholars, and students of every religious and nonreligious conviction. Before the end of Frederic's first spring semester, the group, extremely popular at the Sorbonne, numbered 60 permanent members. But Frederic and Bailly had created a monster. For, as the club debates grew increasingly volatile, atheists and doubters often bested their Catholic hosts. No matter what arguments Catholics raised, their opponents replied: "True, the Church was once a great force for good in this world. But what, my friends, is it doing now?"

One night during hot debate, the articulate Frederic marshaled a finely honed argument concerning Christianity's role in civilization. His adversary waited patiently for Ozanam to conclude and then responded: "Let us be frank, Mr. Ozanam; let us also be very particular. What do you do besides talk to prove the faith you claim is in you?"

The question hit hard and hit home. Frederic, long ago, had promised he would dedicate his talents and energies to defending his faith. So far, the only talent he had really used was his mind, tongue, and ability to lead student protests.

The more Frederic pondered the bitter challenge, the more he determined to answer it. He just did not know how. One evening in early spring, 1833, Frederic finally had his answer. He was convinced God's blessing would not be on his writings, speaking, or organizing until he went to the poor with works of love. He had to back up his words with deeds. "We must do what our Lord Jesus Christ did when preaching the Gospel," he told his friend, Le Taillandier; "we must go to the poor." That very night, Frederic

For the poor, who lived off the streets of Paris, Frederick Ozanam founded the St. Vincent de Paul Society.

and Le Taillandier took their own meager winter wood supply and carried it to a poor family.

Little did the two students realize they were forerunners of a movement that would touch the lives of millions and spread the teachings of Christ far more effectively than any student protest or intellectually stimulating discussion club.

Frederic's heart burst with enthusiasm. Every instinct he possessed told him he had found in the service of the poor the only sure way to fulfill his teenage promise to defend his Catholic faith. His joy was infectious. Five other students joined him and Le Taillandier. Monsieur Bailly and Sister Rosalie, a nun of the Congregation of St. Vincent de Paul, offered to guide the young men. For years, Bailly and his wife visited slum families, quietly helping in whatever way they could, to lighten the brutal burden of the poor.

"You must serve Jesus suffering in the poor man," Bailly warned the boys; "otherwise you will do nothing more for them than the bureaucrats."

Sister Rosalie, a veteran slum worker, provided the boys with lists of families to visit, food to distribute and common sense advice learned from her years in the streets and tenements.

Bailly, Sister Rosalie and the boys met from time to time to reflect on their progress, seek new directions, and to pray. From the very beginning, the little band put their work under the patronage of the great French apostle of charity, St. Vincent de Paul. After all, they were doing the same work Vincent had done nearly two centuries before for their beloved French poor. Bailly reminded the youngsters that, "like St. Vincent, you, too, will find the poor will do much more for you than you will do for them."

The students must have had trouble believing Bailly. Paris' poor

Sister Rosalie Rendue, a Daughter of Charity, was a leader of the first Vincentians and fought the near-overwhelming misery of the poor. Persuasive and compassionate, she had a way of opening the hearts and purses of the rich.

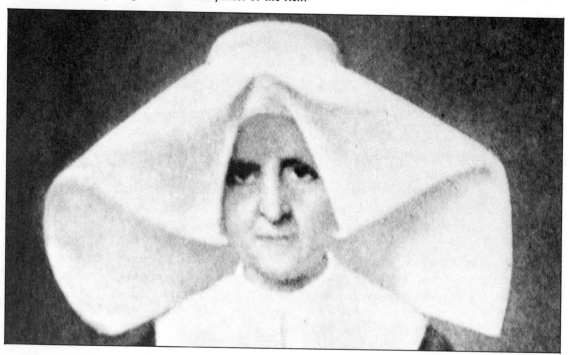

people, exploited by the wealthy, oppressed by the government, were as helpless as any people could be. Those lucky enough to find work, often labored from early morn to late at night, seven days a week, for a miserable salary. Unscrupulous factory owners shamelessly overworked and underpaid little children, who had no laws to protect them. In tenements and alleyways, in twisting cobblestone streets and filthy hallways, drunkenness, vice and immorality flourished. The slums had shortages of food, fuel and fresh air, but no lack of thieves, murderers or procurers—nor tough police to maintain order and keep Paris' prisons well filled.

From time to time all the rage buried within the slums would explode in bloody violence. At the end of Frederic's first year in Paris a frightful riot erupted. Mobs fought each other in Paris' streets, while army and National Guard units attempted to restore order. A cholera epidemic struck, heightening the atmosphere of fear and terror. Disease, death, murder and hatred filled the city's cup of suffering. Before the tragedy ended, municipal authorities were counting 1,500 deaths per day.

It was into these tortured tenement districts, long the focal point of France's troubles, that Frederic and his chums entered with such simplicity and courage. Bailly had warned them not to plan big schemes. "Remember," he counseled, "you are dealing with individuals." With amazing ingenuity the boys responded with what they called "their little works of kindness." A loaf of bread for old Monsieur Chouinard, a few sous to tide over the Widow Oligny, a warm shirt for Monsieur Charbonneau, who was ill. Begging, borrowing and scrounging from every possible source, the students, penniless themselves, always seemed to find what they needed for their poor.

They found something else. A spirit of peace and joy grew among them and bound them together in fraternal love. Ozanam and his group had brought into being a new style of student fraternity and in so doing, had discovered a treasure of fellowship, more delightful because it was unexpected. Old Bailly was right. In the long run the poor did do more for the students than they did for the poor.

* * * * *

Paris in the mid-19th century, where the young Ozanam went to study law and prepare for a career he did not want. Initially he found the city cold and hostile but soon made friends and became intensely involved in defending his faith and helping the poor.

During the next two years, Frederic witnessed the rapid and steady expansion of what came to be known as the St. Vincent de Paul Society. Each new group established was called a "conference" and each new member a "Vincentian." As students returned home from the university they brought the seeds of the Society with them. Soon the movement spread to various corners of France. By the end of 1835, with Bailly's cooperation, Frederic had established a formal rule for the organization.

Although absorbed in his visitation of the poor, Frederic lost no opportunity to encourage France's discouraged Catholics to proclaim their faith more vigorously. It wasn't an easy task. A half century of persecution and harassment had battered the French Catholic Church into timidity. Even the hierarchy was close to losing heart. None of this deterred Frederic, who now came up with a new and exciting plan.

Heading a student delegation of three, Ozanam approached Paris' Archbishop DeQuelen with a petition requesting the prelate to appoint the great French preacher, Father Lacordaire, to the special task of defending the faith from the pulpit of the Notre Dame Cathedral. Aware that Lacordaire had been denounced to the government as a possible revolutionary, and to church authorities as a possible heretic, DeQuelen deferred his decision for more than a year. Eventually the Archbishop relented, and Lacordaire mounted the Notre Dame pulpit in March of 1835 to begin a series of Lenten sermons. Six thousand Frenchmen gathered in the great cathedral to hear the magnificent Lacordaire, "whose words," it was said, "made the cathedral's stone gargoyles weep." To this day, the Archbishop of Paris continues to appoint the best preacher in the land to give the Lenten series Lacordaire initiated and Ozanam inspired.

If Frederic seemed to forget that he originally went to Paris to study law, his father didn't. His parents fretted at all his extracurricular activity, fearing Frederic would ruin his health. They were less than pleased when their son took extra courses in literature. His mother and father were anxious for him to finish his law studies. Finally, in April, 1836, five years after he came to Paris, the Sorbonne granted Frederic the Doctorate in Law. The few students who earned the degree could look forward to rapid advancement in the legal profession. For Frederic, the degree was a sentence of doom in a career he detested. After graduation he returned to his parents' home and began his law practice. It was soon evident he had no stomach for the work. He dutifully carried on, nevertheless, simply to please his father.

One day in May, 1837, Doctor Ozanam, while visiting a patient in a tenement, stumbled on a broken stair and fell, injuring himself fatally. For all the suffering he had caused his son by insisting he become a lawyer, Frederic nevertheless respected him and loved his father. "I owe him this tribute," he wrote; "at least one third of his patients were poor people from whom he refused payment." Within two years Frederic's mother, ill and disheartened by the loss of her husband, also died.

Frederic deeply mourned his loss. His parents had given him priceless gifts of love, provided him with a decent home and fine education, and, above all, offered their children a sterling example of Christian living. Marie, as well as her husband, often visited the poor in Lyons slum areas, doing whatever they could to alleviate their suffering.

Frederic often recalled how, in their old days, both his mother and father, fearing for each other's health, made a mutual pact to climb no higher than the fourth floor of any slum tenement in their work for the poor. Only a short time after this solemn agreement was reached, Jean and Marie met each other accidentally in a garret just under the roof of a tenement that rose high above four stories.

Following his mother's death, Frederic found himself in a peculiar position. At age 26 he had conquered many worlds. Although hardly a success as a practicing attorney, his deep knowledge of law won him the esteemed position of professor of Commercial Law at the University of Lyons.

He had also, in an exercise of extraordinary brilliance, won a second doctorate in literature at the Sorbonne after his father's death in 1837. The young scholar had already published a learned book on the Italian poet Dante that won him international acclaim. And all the while he was engaged in studies, the St. Vincent de Paul Society, numbering 2,000 members, continued to look to Ozanam from every corner of France for guidance.

Despite his near frantic activity and remarkable success, Frederic, alone in this world save for a younger brother, Charles, a student, and an older brother, Alphonse, a priest, was melancholy, depressed and bored.

Frederick's wife Amelie possessed
great intelligence and character.
She was well educated and a talented pianist.
His daughter Marie, a cheerful,
healthy child, was the light of his life.

Once more his old friend, Father Noirot, came to the rescue. "Get married," counseled the priest. His advice fell on deaf ears, for Frederic needed freedom to pursue his many careers. Noirot, not above playing cupid, plotted a "chance meeting" between Frederic and Marie Amelie Soulacroix, daughter of the Rector of the Lyons Academy. On the pretense of introducing Frederic to the rector, Noirot took the youth to the Soulacroix home. As Frederic met the rector, his eye wandered to a windowsill in the corner of the room. There, surrounded by the early morning sunlight, a beautiful girl sat tending her crippled brother with such good cheer and affection that Ozanam's heart broke with tenderness. So absorbed was the girl in her brother that she didn't notice Frederic. But he noticed her and begged to meet her. Good-bye loneliness, good-bye boredom, good-bye freedom. Perhaps no one observed the small smile on Noirot's face as, concluding his visit, he left Frederic and returned to his professor's study.

On June 23, 1841, Father Alphonse Ozanam witnessed the marriage of his brother Frederic to Amelie Soulacroix in the church of St. Nizier in Lyons. Although a typical absentminded professor, Frederic never forgot this date. On the 23rd of each month of their marriage, he always presented Amelie with a bouquet of flowers.

* * * * *

A few months before his marriage to Amelie, Sorbonne authorities requested Frederic to join their faculty as a Professor of Literature. Ozanam was honored and delighted by the appointment. Paris was his spiritual home, and the nerve center of the St. Vincent de Paul movement. Further, the Sorbonne was a university enjoying world fame. He and Amelie settled in an apartment near the Luxembourg Gardens and Frederic began a teaching career that was to win him honors, love, respect and not a few tears.

Neither handsome, elegant, nor particularly graceful, afflicted by nearsightedness and hair that refused to be tamed, Frederic's professorial appearance left something to be desired. That is, until one looked at his face. It was full of light, simple refinement, and cheerful exuberance.

His students revered him. His love of literature was so powerful that it could smash the shell of boredom in which most students had encased them-

While teaching at the Sorbonne, Ozanam published a
moving study of Franciscan poetry.
Like Francis of Assisi, he saw creation as the manifestation
of God's beauty, a sign of his love.

selves. Ozanam's lectures were masterpieces of oratory. "He prepared like
a monk," a friend remarked. "He had the secret fire," another noted. Alive,
lighthearted and learned, Frederic could crack-up a class with his humor or
bring them to tears as he, himself weeping, would lay bare the beauty of a
literary masterpiece.

Fearlessly he proclaimed Catholicism from his professor's chair. More
than one student, moved by the learning and simple faith of Ozanam, rejected
the Sorbonne's cold atheism, and returned to the faith of his fathers.

The young professor had a knack for bringing out the best in all his
students. He was particularly concerned about the dull ones. Once, following
an introductory lecture, Ozanam sought out the student who occupied last
rank in the class. The youngster, used to scorn, derision and, even worse,
condescension from his teachers, steeled himself for some sarcasm from the

great Ozanam. Instead, the professor took time to patiently go over every detail of the lecture until he was sure the boy grasped it. The next day Ozanam received a note from the young fellow. "I promise you most faithfully that I shall show my gratitude to you by achieving the impossible," the boy wrote. At the end of the school year, the dunce achieved the impossible. He earned first prize in general excellence. Subsequently this young man became a professor.

Frederic continued to rally Sorbonne Catholic students and encouraged them to join the St. Vincent de Paul movement. By now, Paris claimed 25 conferences, and their charitable works drew much attention. Fearing that the larger organization might lose the spirit of simplicity so characteristic of the Society's early days, Frederic warned: "God is pleased to bless this tiny and inconspicuous group. We must not hamper our progress with too much organization and red tape."

*   *   *   *   *

"After a succession of favors, yet another is added," Frederic wrote to a friend in August, 1845, "probably the greatest we can have on earth: I am a father. . . ." Ozanam's tender, gentle heart, thrilled with sheer joy and delight when he looked over the cradle at his new baby daughter, Marie, born in August, 1845. Well it was that the professor experienced such deep joy, for only a year after Marie's birth, Ozanam, worn out by all the teaching, writing, research and Vincentian work, fell severely ill and almost died.

Skilled physicians pulled him through, but the fever he suffered left him weak, and enervated. Frederic did not convalesce well; as soon as he gathered any strength at all, he would try to study or write. Invariably the effort exhausted him. "An hour's light work," he complained, "and I am finished." Even in these straits he could neither forget nor resist his poor. Although unable to make his visits, Ozanam ordered a supply of fresh bread for the poor who came to visit him. As they were leaving, Ozanam would offer them the bread and beg for their prayers.

University authorities, concerned lest they should lose Ozanam completely, suggested the professor take a year's leave of absence and pursue

The French were split into two mutually hostile camps in 1848—the moneyed and the workers. In May the workers seized the French National Assembly. Bloody fighting in the streets followed.

literary research in Italy. Grateful for the opportunity, Frederic, Amelie and Marie left Paris in August, 1846. As the little family traveled through Italy's lovely cities and villages, Frederic visited not only libraries, but parish houses as well. In Italy's libraries he mined the rich treasure of Italian literature; but in the parishes he planted the seeds of the St. Vincent de Paul Society. It wasn't long after this tour that the Society took firm root in Italy.

Returning to Paris in August, 1847, Frederic experienced a sense of impending doom for France. The forces of hatred, injustice, greed and violence that lay just under the polished surface of French society were gathering like the fires of an underground volcano.

"It is a struggle," Frederic noted, "between those who have nothing and those who have too much. The violent clash of luxury and poverty is shaking the ground under our feet."

In February, 1848, the first eruption occurred. Revolutionary mobs of unemployed workers broke into the Tuileries Palace, vandalizing it and setting fires. During the rioting, a young Vincentian rushed to the palace chapel to rescue the Blessed Sacrament from the mobs. A clutch of rioters spotted the youth leaving the chapel and immediately paused and surrounded him. The Vincentian froze in fear. But when the hard-eyed vandals discovered the young man was not stealing the Eucharist but only attempting to protect it, they immediately formed an honor guard to accompany him through the riot to a nearby church.

As the little procession progressed through the streets, the workers shouted, "Long live liberty! Long live the Catholic Faith!" Arriving at the church, the men knelt down before the parish priest and requested his blessing. The poor and the workers did not wish to abandon the church. It is a sad footnote to French history that so many French clergy could not believe that and refused to labor among the nation's working classes.

Eventually the February rioting came to an end, only to break out with new and terrible force on June 24, 1848. This time the government determined to grind the Revolutionaries into powder. Like a great bear eating off its own foot to escape a trap, the French nation, at that time one of the world's wealthiest, turned to destroy its own people in an insane attempt to escape the trap of injustice and greed which it had forged for itself.

Over 100,000 armed rebels rampaged through Paris in the first hours of the June fighting. But the insurgents, without leadership, strategy or resources, were no match for the better equipped, trained and disciplined government troops. Soon government forces drove their opponents behind the makeshift stone barricades. From there the rebels, although outmanned and outgunned, refused to retreat any farther and fought it out, preferring to die rather than starve. Ozanam, still weak from his illness, nevertheless felt duty-bound to respond when he was called up for the National Guard, as were 800,000 other Frenchmen. He bade Amelie and Marie good-bye. "It was a terrible moment," he remembered; "I thought I would never see them again."

It was a week of terrible moments. Frederic suffered bitter anguish as he saw his Parisian poor so mercilessly and methodically cut down. On the third day of the fighting, Ozanam and two of his comrades approached Archbishop Affre with a plan to stop the slaughter. Ozanam inquired if the Archbishop would be willing to approach the insurgents and offer them a promised government pardon. The prelate, whose heart, too, was broken by the madness that gripped his people, was only too willing to comply. General Cavaignac, commanding the government army, advised the Archbishop that a pardon could indeed be arranged, but that approaching the rebel barricades was dangerous. Only the day before, Cavaignac had sent one of his generals under a flag of truce to parley with the rebels. The insurgents, refusing to honor the truce flag, imprisoned the officer. Archbishop Affre listened politely and, when the general concluded, simply said, "I must go."

As the Archbishop left Cavaignac's headquarters and proceeded through government lines, soldiers, sensing his mission, leaped to attention and saluted him. The prelate stopped briefly to bless the wounded and then walked deliberately and without hesitation past the last government outpost and into the no-man's-land between the two lines. As he did so, a young Vincentian climbed high in a tree to raise a white handkerchief of truce. Firing from the barricades lessened and then ceased.

Affre pressed on through the strangely silent streets. No one spoke, no one moved. A thousand eyes watched the brave Archbishop. A thousand breaths came shorter as he approached the barricades. He seemed so small, so helpless. After an eternity Affre reached the front of the main rebel barricade. Insurgents came from behind their fortress to greet him. The Archbishop read a beautiful statement of reconciliation, and then in gentle tones urged the rebels to accept the pardon. The workers' hearts were deeply touched and they sat silent. Suddenly a shot rang out, and within moments a frightful firefight erupted. Affre was cut down and mortally wounded. Rebel soldiers, braving a hail of government bullets, dragged the Archbishop's broken body behind the barricades.

The insurgents took the dying Archbishop to a nearby parish house, and early next morning Affre died. "May my blood be the last to be shed," was the final prayer the humble hero uttered.

The news of Affre's death was enough to stop the insane fighting, which by now claimed 10,000 killed and wounded. At first Frederic and his companions felt terrible remorse. After all, it was at their suggestion that Affre took his last desperate journey. But the more they pondered the Archbishop's magnificent courage the more they felt that Affre gladly gave his life to stop the frightful slaughter.

Despite the bloodletting and great promises, French social conditions failed to improve following the revolution. No one yet seemed to realize that unless justice and charity prevailed in the land, the nation would inevitably destroy itself. The 1848 revolution's aftermath left 267,000 workmen unemployed in Paris. Companies and corporations, factories and businesses, having already suffered heavy losses, refused to reopen in the politically unstable city. Paris without commerce, business or money, was once more paralyzed.

The city, lacking any resources, could not care for its sick, its children or its poor. Trust between France's moneyed and laboring classes broke down almost completely. The workmen and poor felt they were duped into the June surrender; the upper classes refused to make even a show of compassion or forgiveness for the revolt. Paris' poorer classes had no work, no credit, no food and, worst of all, no hope.

St. Vincent de Paul members threw themselves tirelessly into their slum work. Frederic, using every bit of influence he had, obtained help from every quarter to relieve the sufferings of the poor. The government collected enough money to provide a small assistance for the city's poor.

"We must do what our Lord Jesus Christ did when preaching the Gospel," Frederick said. *"We must go to the poor."*

In factories and workshops resentment and rage built in the hearts of the workers.
Politicians traveled and professors pronounced, but still the working poor suffered.

It requested Ozanam and his men to supervise the distribution of this fund. By this time, the Vincentians had spread beyond France to other European nations, and conferences of many lands sent funds for French relief. Particularly touching was the money sent from Ireland, which had so many troubles of its own.

As if poor Paris did not suffer enough, a cholera epidemic struck the city near the end of 1848. The Vincentians joined the Sisters of Charity in tending the thousands of sick and dying in the tenements. Ozanam, the gallant warrior and gentle poet, walked through the streets of his beloved, bewildered, and bedeviled Paris. The faith of his poor, who faced death so courageously and asked nothing more than that a priest be with them to close their eyes, moved him to tears.

*   *   *   *   *

Although depressed by the endless political wrangling, the prattling of intellectuals, the timidity and blindness of the French clergy, Frederic was not yet ready to surrender hope. He began publishing a newspaper whose policy was to secure justice for the poor and working classes. He called the paper *The New Era*. His enemies entitled it *The New Error*.

Many fellow Catholics, angry with Frederic because of his gentleness and genuine compassion for the church's enemies, accused him in print and in public speech, of compromise, timidity, and even complicity in anti-Catholic efforts. The charges tore the nearly exhausted Frederic apart. "All my life I have followed the poetry of love in preference to the poetry of anger," he explained; "I will not change now."

A sensitive, dedicated man, Frederic could not believe fellow Christians would so unjustly and venomously attack him. Meanwhile, in *The New Era,* he continued to stir the conscience of the French people. He reminded his readers that France owed assistance to the poor, not an assistance that humiliated but an assistance that honored. In Frederic's eyes the poor man could pray for the rich and in this way give more than he received. Ozanam reminded France that the poor man was the nation's priest. His hunger, his sweat, his blood constituted a sacrifice which could redeem the

people's broken humanity. In his newspaper Frederic continually warned
that if the French government continued to ignore the needs of the poor it
would drive them back into the arms of those who led them into the June
upheaval. Frederic lost patience with those intellectuals who tirelessly propagated social programs to alleviate the sufferings of the poor. "Social welfare reform is to be learned," Frederic admonished, "not in books or from
a public platform but in climbing the stairs to a poor man's garret, sitting by
his bedside, feeling the same cold that pierces him, sharing the secrets of his
lonely heart and troubled mind."

                    *   *   *   *   *

Until the spring of 1850 Frederic continued his struggle to bring
peace and justice to his own people. Laboring in the classroom, at the editor's
desk, visiting the poor, lecturing, writing, and doing his scholarly research,
Frederic soon consumed the small resources of strength he had. As his physical health began once more to deteriorate, he realized that the hatreds un-
leashed by the 1848 revolution would not be healed. The passions were too
bitter, the resentments implacable. "It is full time God let light into this
chaos," he prayed. All his work began now to appear so futile. Depression
dogged him. "I had thought I had some ideas," he wrote, "and some work
to do in this world. I'm afraid I have greatly overestimated myself."

The illness that plagued him for the past few years struck and struck
again. Fever inexorably destroyed his strength.

Just after Easter, 1852, doctors ordered him to surrender his teaching
post at the Sorbonne. Summoning all his strength and in a clear, resonant
voice, Frederic delivered his last lecture. As he concluded, his students, overcome with emotion, clapped, cheered and wept all at the same time. The
Sorbonne would never see his like again and everyone knew it.

In July doctors ordered him once more to southern Europe, where
they hoped the sea air and warm climate would restore his strength. And
once more the little Ozanam family made its way to southern France, de-
toured briefly into Spain, and finally arrived in Italy. During this painful
journey, Frederic, although suffering from swelling feet, weakening heart,

and the ever-present fever, never lost his sense of humor. Arriving at Pisa, he noted, "I am like this city's famous tower, leaning but not quite falling."

Leaning and near falling though he was, Frederic managed at every turn of this year-long journey to establish new Vincentian groups wherever he went. As the spring of 1853 broke, Ozanam, Amelie and Marie moved to a tiny seaside cottage on the Mediterranean coast. The love between Amelie and himself grew deeper and more tender as each day passed. The couple often sat for hours in silence contemplating the clear blue skies and sparkling Mediterranean Sea. As spring ripened, the poet within him sensed death was near. "April smiles," he wrote, "but to deceive."

Area fishermen and farm folk came to love the gentle, thoughtful Frenchman. Each day they brought him baskets of his favorite flowers as

well as fresh fish and fruit. With remarkable Italian ingenuity, the people found ice even in the summer to keep his fever down. Frederic had opened his heart to the poor of France, and now as he was dying, the poor of Italy filled his last days with great love and peace. As summer waned he yearned to see once more his beloved Paris. In late August his two brothers, Charles the doctor and Alphonse the priest, arrived at the seaside cottage to assist him home. The family set departure for the end of August.

Before Frederic left the cottage he had one more task to accomplish. He had spotted a myrtle tree in flower on the seashore. With an effort that must have drained his last bit of strength, he cut some of the beautiful

During his last two years of life, Frederic's health slowly disintegrated. *"Illness,"* he complained, *"makes me irritable and selfish. God grant to make me holy."*

flowers and arranged a bouquet for Amelie. It was, after all, the 23rd of the month, their wedding anniversary, and there are some things a gallant Frenchman never forgets.

In early September the Ozanam entourage reached Marseilles, France, where Amelie's mother came to meet them. The Ozanams' relatives had prepared a house for him to stay in Marseilles on his way to Paris.

Immediately after his arrival in Marseilles the exhausted Frederic took to his bed. He was at peace. "Now that I have placed Amelie in your arms," he remarked to his mother-in-law, "God will do with me what he will."

Lacordaire, writing of these last hours of his friend's life said: "He spoke little but he had a pressure of the hand, a smile, a sign for those whom he loved. Feeling his end approaching, he himself asked for the last sacraments. As the priest who attended him enjoined him to entrust himself to the goodness of God without fear, Frederic replied, "Ah, why should I fear him? I love him so."

On the eighth of September, the feast of the birthday of the Blessed Mother, Frederic, surrounded by his family and with his brother Alphonse reciting the prayers for the dying, left this world to meet his Lord. Those who knew him were sure it was no meeting of strangers. Lacordaire, who had fought shoulder to shoulder with Frederic to restore Catholicism to France, best described his friend in his eulogy at the funeral in Paris. "Ozanam," the mighty preacher declared, "was one of those privileged creatures who came direct from the hand of God, in whom God joins tenderness to genius in order to enkindle the world."

At his death in 1853, the St. Vincent de Paul Society which he had started with Le Taillandier numbered 15,000 "brothers," as they were called. Today Vincentians, numbering nearly 700,000, are found in every quarter of the globe, carrying on a multitude of charitable works. Surely their charity is the greatest monument to the life of Frederic Ozanam.

The cause for Frederic Ozanam's beatification was formally introduced in 1953.

4. Maximilian Kolbe

Auschwitz was a circle of hell on the face of the earth. It was a concentration camp where the Nazis, shortly after their invasion of Poland in September, 1939, held political prisoners of all religions and beliefs contrary to their own.

In Auschwitz cell block 14, during the night of July 30, 1941, prisoners spread the dreaded word: "Someone has escaped." The rumor left inmates numb with horror, for they knew what was about to happen. Their Nazi captors would take hostages, and 10 men would pay with their lives for each escaped prisoner.

The Nazis, discovering the loss of their prisoner at morning roll call, quickly executed vengeance. They ordered all cell block 14 inmates to stand at full attention in the camp yard. The men, weakened by months of imprisonment and inhuman treatment, stood rigidly in the broiling sunlight for several hours without food and water. One by one they fainted. At half-past three, the guards allowed the unfortunates a bit of rest and gave them some thin soup and water. For 10 prisoners it was their last meal on earth.

As the sun set, the Nazis began the dreadful process of selecting the

Kolbe, a prisoner of the
Nazis at Auschwitz.

doomed. An Auschwitz survivor wrote:
"During my two years at Auschwitz,
I stood about a dozen lineups like this.
I never really got used to them, but
after a while a man just got numb. The
worst was when I was standing in the
front row. The commandant of the
camp, in selecting the hostages, pointed
at me—so I thought! It was the most
frightful moment of suffering I ever
lived through. It turned out that he
was pointing at the man behind me.
These poor hostages were sentenced to
starve to death."

And now, on this warm July
evening, Gestapo Commandant Fritsch
was selecting 10 innocent men to die
of starvation. Quickly Fritsch chose
his 10, ordered them to step forward
and march to the underground bunker,
where they would be locked until hunger and thirst claimed them.

Suddenly, Sergeant Francis Gajowniczek, one of Fritsch's choices,
burst out in tears: "My poor wife and
children! I will never see them again."

The men of cell block 14
watched the grotesque proceeding with
feelings of both horror and relief. They
now stood immobile, frozen in fear.
All but one. He strode purposefully
from the prisoners' ranks and stepped

Kolbe confronts his captors.

before the commandant. "I would like," he said softly, "to take the place of Sergeant Gajowniczek."

Commander Fritsch scrutinized the inmate standing before him, a frail man in his forties. The sufferings of concentration camp life and illness had ravaged his body. There was about him, however, a compelling aura of calm and peace. During his career as ruler of this empire of death, Fritsch had seen many things but never before had he encountered someone willing to give his life for another prisoner.

"Who are you?" the Nazi asked. "I am a Catholic priest," the inmate replied.

For Fritsch there was no problem as long as he had 10 hostages. And so the commandant ordered the priest, whose name was Father Maximilian Kolbe, to take Gajowniczek's place in the starvation bunker.

As the prisoners marched toward the death cells they could hear the howls of torment, the curses, screams, and groans of despair emanating from other starvation bunkers in the death area. Now Nazi gun butts drove the men of cell block 14 into their death cell. The steel doors clanked shut, sealing them in. A prison guard gloated at the prisoners as they entered; "You will come out like dried-up tulip bulbs."

But this bunker, No. 11, at Auschwitz, was destined to become like no other torture chamber in the camp. The little priest made the difference. Gradually, under his calm guidance and control, the men began to pray. Although they were on the rim of hatred and despair, the priest managed to help them sustain their faith in God. At Father Kolbe's urging, they turned to the Blessed Mother to keep them from degrading into the animals the Nazis wanted them to be.

Bruno Borgowiec, an Auschwitz inmate assigned to remove dead bodies from the death bunkers, testified under oath:

> In one bunker was Father Kolbe. The cell, with the cold and the cement floor, had no window and no furniture. Just a pail for natural needs. The stench was overwhelming. Father never complained. He prayed aloud, so that his fellow prisoners could hear him in order to join him. He had the special gift of comforting everybody. When his fellow prisoners, writhing in agony, were begging for a drop of water, and in despair were screaming and cursing, Father Kolbe would calm them down, inspiring them to perseverance.

The calmness and serenity of Father Kolbe's face and eyes so overwhelmed the Nazi guards that they refused to look at him. "Look at the ground!" his captors shouted. "Don't look at us."

As the men entered the third week in the bunker, only Father Kolbe and three others survived. The Nazis, now impatient to kill them, ordered Bock, the camp executioner, to inject the remaining four men with carbolic acid. On August 14, the eve of the feast of the Assumption, Bock murdered the remaining four.

Their bodies were taken to the camp crematorium and burned. Someone later remembered that Father Kolbe had often said to his fellow Franciscans: "I hope that after my death nothing remains of me and that the winds blow my dust away over the whole world."

* * * * *

Who was this remarkable priest? What is his story? Of what stuff was he made that he could offer his life with such courage on that fateful July night? What caliber of man could lead other men to choose serenity, calmness and faith in place of hatred and despair in the circumstances of a cruel death deliberately provoked by his fellowmen; not a quick death, but a hideous death brought about by willfully withholding food and water?

Perhaps Pope Paul VI, in speaking of Father Kolbe, can best describe our sentiments. The Pope, in October, 1971, remarked:

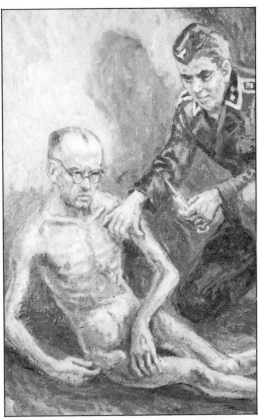

The picture of the ending of this man's life is so horrible and harrowing that we would prefer not to speak about it, not to contemplate it anymore, in order not to see what lengths may be reached by inhuman arrogance. . . , but history cannot forget this frightful page. And so it cannot but fix its horrified gaze on the luminous points that not only reveal but actually overcome its inconceivable darkness.

One of these points, perhaps the one that glows most brightly, is the calm, exalted figure of Maximilian Kolbe. His name will remain among the great. . . .

After three weeks of starvation, the Nazis killed Father Kolbe by injecting him with carbolic acid.

And so the little priest who is known to the world as Father Maximilian Kolbe, O.F.M. Conv., who desired nothing else than to disappear at death completely into God, today is very much alive. The dust of his memory has been charged with light and is gradually suffusing the world. As Christ rose out of the earth to lead men to new hope, so the memory of Father Maximilian Kolbe has risen from the dreaded bunker at Auschwitz to remind men that the work of Christ continues.

Father Maximilian's death, with the intense generosity and Christian love that characterized it, was only the final act of a life filled with great hope, great love and, above all, great faith.

He was born January 7, 1894, in Zdunska Wola, Poland. His parents, Julius and Maryanne, named their second son Raymond. He was baptized in the parish church of the Assumption of Our Lady.

Raymond, a youngster charged with energy, was quickly turning Mrs. Kolbe's hair gray by his pranks and escapades. One day she chided her little son: "Raymie, what will become of you?" The mother's query triggered something within the boy. He suddenly became more serious-minded and obedient at home and began to spend more time in prayer. The mother, delighted, puzzled, and worried all at the same time, as most mothers would be at such a change, did not quite know how to handle it. Finally Mrs. Kolbe

Father Kolbe took Francis Gajowniczek's place in the starvation bunker.

asked Raymie just what was going on. The little boy responded: "After you asked me what would become of me, I prayed to the Blessed Mother and asked her what will become of me."

The little boy then said that the Blessed Mother offered him two crowns, a white one and a red one. "She asked me which one of these crowns I wanted," little Raymond explained, "the white one signifying that I will persevere in purity and the red one that I will be a martyr. I told Mary that I wanted them both."

We can only imagine how Mrs. Kolbe felt after that conversation.

In the year 1907, when he was 13, Raymie entered the Franciscan minor seminary in Lwow. Seminary professors were delighted with his intelligence, his talent for mathematics and physics, and predicted great things for young Kolbe.

As a teenager, Raymond's vision was deep and his horizons extremely broad. He had a profound and disciplined interest in space and seriously planned space travel apparatus. And this before World War I!

At this point Raymie had not definitely decided to become a Franciscan friar. He appreciated his own inventive talents. Totally absorbed in love of his country, he felt he might best serve Poland as a military officer. Now approaching his sixteenth year, Kolbe would soon have to decide which path of life to follow.

Finally, and not without pain, he chose to enter the Franciscan Order.

In 1910 Raymond Kolbe entered the Franciscan Order and re-

Father Kolbe's mother, Maria, in 1941.

ceived his new name, Brother Maximilian. Immediately following the youth's first profession, his superiors sent Brother Maximilian to study philosophy and theology in Rome. The Eternal City's cosmopolitan atmosphere broke open the provincial mold of the young Pole. The young Franciscan realized that there were men and women suffering because of the evil that pervaded so much of the Western world. He found, too, that there were men who had never heard of Christ, or cared very much about him.

Something else happened to Raymond in Rome. He became very deeply interested in the Blessed Mother's role in the work of salvation. He applied his enormous intelligence in a struggle to comprehend Mary and her meaning. Indeed he questioned whether Mary had any vital role to play in the healing of men and in the rescuing of the human race from evil and its horrifying effects on individuals and society. Was Mary simply the sweet and delightful Mother who really had a secondary position as far as the happiness and eternal destiny of the human race were concerned?

This area of theology totally absorbed young Brother Maximilian. The mystery of Mary eventually would dominate his whole life. Already he began to perceive God's Mother as the divinely chosen agent through whom the tide of darkness gradually and inexorably gathering about the twentieth-century world, could be reversed. The young friar now dedicated himself to her service and, because of his military cast of mind, dubbed himself her knight. For the first time, as far as we know, he began to think of himself

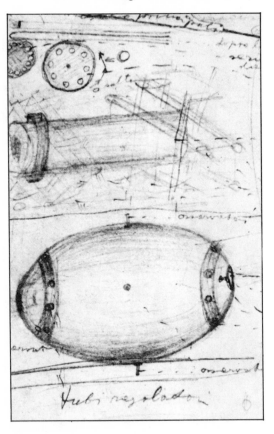

Enthralled by the idea of space travel, Kolbe sketched a spaceship.

as "the knight" of Mary, the Immaculate Mother.

Stirred by an interior vision that saw Mary as Queen of the Universe, Maximilian began to express outwardly his deep conviction of Mary's role in human society. He writes: "This is the age of the Blessed Virgin; now begins the era of Mary Immaculate. Mary is the Mother, the real Mother, of each one of us . . . and the Queen of Society. We must practically recognize Mary's mission as Queen and Mother, then let her act fully, freely; she will then have unheard-of triumphs; she will conquer every enemy."

His keen intelligence perceived the signs of the times. The forces of evil were gathering, the fist of war forming. It would drop quickly on the world in two sledgehammer blows—World War I and World War II.

Maximilian's life was framed by these two horrible events. And yet, as this tide of evil ebbed and flowed over our world and convulsed it in pain and indescribable agony, Maximilian never ceased to believe that the power of God was still at work. With all his heart, he felt that, through Mary, Christ was continuing his saving work for the human race and that the healing of society through the Immaculate Mother was becoming more and more a reality. Before his ordination in Rome, the young Franciscan, with the approval of his superiors, organized a group of friars into what he called "The Knights of Mary Immaculate."

This little group, reminiscent of Francis of Assisi's Knights of the Round Table, dedicated themselves to win for Mary, by word, example and prayer, nothing less than the whole world. The first circle was organized October 17, 1917. It was just a year before the end of World War I.

Maximilian was ordained a priest on April 28, 1918. The following year his superiors sent him to the Franciscan Seminary in Cracow, Poland. Here Father Kolbe taught philosophy and church history, and continued his work as a Knight of Mary.

Gradually the young professor gathered about him people, religious and lay, devoted to Mary. He organized them into what he termed the "M. I.," the Militia of the Immaculate. The objective of this militia was the same as that of the Knights of Mary Immaculate he had established while in Rome; to conquer the whole world for Mary. Kolbe's army believed in violence, but only in violence to the Knights' own selfishness and self-will.

Maximilian's ambition was staggering—and completely Franciscan. He had nothing but absolute trust in God, Mary, and his fellowman.

Already he was planning to reach the masses of humanity through the press and radio. Sensitive to technology's potential, Maximilian saw the new and marvelous discoveries as vehicles for bringing the messages of Mary and her role in the healing of the broken human race to the knowledge and the hearts of men. No dreamer, Father Kolbe, in January, 1922, instituted a monthly magazine called *The Knight of the Immaculate*. During the 20's and early 30's, many magazines appeared throughout the Catholic world, but none entered the publishing field surrounded with the absolute poverty of *The Knight*. No "knight" ever went into combat so ill-equipped. Maximilian had no financial backing, could not even secure a loan, and Poland at the time was gripped in a fierce financial depression. His Franciscan colleagues gave him little support or comfort. They felt the magazine would die in infancy. His superiors, somewhat reluctantly, permitted the new project, despite the depressing times. Father Kolbe, to everyone's amazement, managed to keep afloat financially.

*   *   *   *   *

From his student days in Rome, when he suffered from tuberculosis, deplorable health plagued Maximilian. So sickly was he upon his return to Poland after his ordination that Kolbe's superiors felt he would live no more than a few months. Even at this stage of his career, illness caused difficulty in his breathing and slowed his pace. He experienced frequent hemorrhaging. Witless confreres dubbed him "Marmalade" because of the slowness of his movements.

Friars of the Cracow monastery dedicated themselves to the traditional works of hearing confessions, preaching, saying Mass, attending the sick, and so forth. When Father Kolbe, a relatively young priest, arrived with his impractical dream of publishing a seemingly meaningless magazine, he hardly fit into their orderly scheme. Although Maximilian was a devoted religious and fulfilled the common prayer life conscientiously, the ceaseless activity, the accompanying bustle, and the business of the press upset the Cracow friary.

The friars were too well aware that Kolbe had initiated the magazine only after obtaining the superiors' reluctant permission. He went into debt to purchase supplies and mailing equipment for his first issue. No one helped him with its writing, proofreading or composition. For Americans who spend most of their lives in debt, it is difficult to realize that for a European friar, this was a frightful and almost sinful condition. When Maximilian, then, went into debt and could not find money to pay it off, his provincial superiors turned a cold eye toward him.

In effect, his superior said, "We did not ask you to start this, and we are not going to bail you out." The provincial and the friars of Kolbe's Cracow community looked upon the whole situation as the zeal of a young priest outrunning his common sense.

But, as always, God uses saints to prove that his ways are not man's ways. Two sources came to Maximilian's assistance in this first financial crisis. A parish priest in Cracow, moved by the simplicity and purpose of Maximilian's work, donated most generously and unexpectedly toward the magazine. This helped pay a good part of the debt, but still the priest-publisher needed more to finally pay it off.

With nowhere to turn, Kolbe knelt before the Blessed Mother's altar at St. Francis Basilica in Cracow. During his prayers, the young priest became oblivious to everything; and then, as he concluded, he rose and noticed on Mary's altar a small envelope. He went to the altar, picked up the enve-

Kolbe as a young Franciscan.

lope. and saw written on it, "For you, O Immaculate Mother." Maximilian opened the envelope and found in it the exact sum that he owed his creditors.

Eventually, the provincial authorities transferred Father Maximilian to Grodno, on Poland's eastern border. Here, things improved greatly for him and his work. The provincial assigned a brother to help him, and between Father Kolbe and Brother Melchior a deep bond of friendship grew as, together, they pioneered their little magazine.

But business conditions did not improve during the 20's in Poland. Five times during the first year, Maximilian changed printers to meet continually rising prices. He finally decided to purchase his own printing press. Again, in an almost miraculous way, money appeared.

Because of the financial depression, Father Maximilian had difficulty gathering funds. One evening an American Franciscan provincial joined the friary recreation at Grodno. Maximilian's companions were poking fun at him for fund-raising in these hard times. The American provincial listened. The American temper flared slightly, and the friar chided his Franciscan brethren: "You ought to help this man instead of ridiculing him." To back up his words, the provincial made a generous donation to Maximilian's press. It was one of the best foreign-aid investments ever made.

Despite the fact of the bad Polish economy, Father Kolbe quickly gathered enough funds to purchase the press. Another friar joined his editorial staff. The three Franciscans now set to work writing, setting type, printing, and distributing the 5,000 copies of *The Knight*.

Besides all this work, Father Kolbe was assigned to parish duties at Grodno. Not a physically strong man, he accepted these extra and seemingly unfair burdens without complaint. He fulfilled them enthusiastically. His two companions also had friary assignments and Kolbe insisted that they fulfill them. Thus it was not unusual for the three of them to work by day in the friary and parish, and all night long on the magazine.

Circulation of *The Knight* increased by leaps and bounds. Maximilian now had to purchase a Linotype machine for setting type. Not one of the friars publishing *The Knight* knew the first thing about a Linotype. Maximilian's confreres, judging the purchase of the expensive machine as another folly, showered a small storm of ridicule on the poor friar. But they

From his large and cluttered room, Father Kolbe conducted his press work.
His publications reached millions in all parts of the world.

forgot for whom the young priest was working. It was Mary, and she soon showed her appreciation. Immediately after the Linotype's arrival, a young mechanic knocked on the friary door at Grodno and asked admittance to the order. The youth was a highly trained specialist and soon had the Linotype humming away happily, pounding out type for Maximilian's publication.

More and more brothers came to join the publishing enterprise, and soon the group formed a community within the Franciscan community at Grodno. Production of the little magazine within three of the worst depression years in Poland soared from 5,000 to 45,000 copies per issue. In five years it reached 70,000, while the Militia of the Immaculate numbered 126,000 members.

The strain, however, proved too much for Kolbe, and once more tuberculosis struck and forced him into a sanitarium.

Maximilian must now have suffered some deep sense of frustration. His work was just beginning to bear fruit. His militia was now paying for itself. His work of teaching about the Blessed Mother and promoting Marian devotion through the magazine was proceeding very effectively. But now he was ill. Realizing he could now best serve through his suffering, Kolbe accepted the illness with his profound sense of calmness and patience. Doctors released him after some months in the sanitarium, and he returned to pursue a new and bold project.

By 1927, circulation of *The Knight* increased to 60,000, and Maximilian had to find a new location for his publishing enterprise. The priest discovered a large property, a forest near Warsaw, belonging to a Polish prince. The prince, moved by the religious spirit of Maximilian and the purposes of his work, generously gave the property to the Franciscans.

Maximilian moved the friars and their equipment to this new location in October, 1927. Cutting the forest's raw timber, the friars constructed a chapel, sleeping quarters, equipment huts, workshops, and administrative offices. These early pioneering days were very trying. The Polish winter came early and severely. But the friars were strong men, and adversity brought out the best in them. Their dedication to their work and its purpose forged a tremendous bond of love, joy, and cheer between Maximilian and these other sons of St. Francis.

By now, tuberculosis had destroyed a portion of Kolbe's lungs. Although he hemorrhaged frequently, he would permit himself no privileges but indeed led in the energetic prosecution of this work.

Wise men must have shaken their heads when they saw the ragged little group of men building their dream in the cold forest outside the gates of Warsaw. What brought them together, what kept them working, what developed among them in the midst of so many contrary currents, can only be explained as the movement of God's grace in this forgotten corner of the world.

Incredible things happened in that forest of the Polish prince. Building by building, the City of the Immaculate, as the friars called this place, grew. The original community of two priests and 17 lay brothers who arrived in 1927 grew within a decade to 762 Conventual friars. Thirteen of these friars were priests. Every brother was a specialist in some field of modern communications. The area, known as Niepokalanow, boasted the largest religious community of men in the world.

As the first decade passed, building after building grew from the forest floor. During the first five years they constructed a chapel, a college, a novitiate, a friary for professed Franciscans, a 100-bed hospital, an electric plant, and a fire department. A short time after this, a radio station was erected, and then an airport begun.

This external growth was only a reflection of the personal development and growth in the spirit of the friars under Maximilian's direction. He realized that this tremendous burst of energy could produce wealth, and this, he knew, would destroy his friars and their work. Any hint of financial profit repelled him. He made it clear that if the friars ever worked for any other aim than the service of Mary, he would separate himself from their work.

On the eve of the outbreak of World War II, *The Knight*'s circulation had increased to almost a million copies per issue. Besides this, Maximilian's presses were offering no less than nine different publications, varying from a spiritual magazine in Latin for priests to an illustrated periodical called *The Sporting Journal*.

"All progress is spiritual," Father Kolbe taught, "or it is not progress." The foundation of the City of the Immaculate rested on the holiness of life of the Franciscans gathered there. With discerning simplicity, Father Kolbe made clear the only formula for their success: "We ourselves must first be holy."

"The true Niepokalanow," he explained, "is in our hearts. Everything else is only secondary." A dialogue between Father Kolbe and one of his confreres has survived the years. It echoes the famous conversation between Francis and Brother Leo.

"Tell us, Father, in what does true progress in our work consist?" the brother questioned the superior. "It is in being poor, without our own resources," Father Kolbe replied.

In lyrical phrases that twentieth-century followers of St. Francis can well understand, Father Kolbe goes on: "If we were to have the latest machines, if we were to use all technical improvements and all discoveries

Maximilian and his friars worked steadily and swiftly and within a decade had constructed the City of the Immaculate. Production facilities housed some of the best available printing equipment.

of modern science, this would not yet be true progress. If our magazines doubled and even tripled their circulation, that would not be true progress."

"What, then, is necessary, Father," the brother asked, "to have true progress here in our work?" Without hesitation, the priest answered: "Our exterior activity, whether in the friary or outside it, does not constitute Niepokalanow. Even if all members of the militia abandon us, even if all our magazine circulation went to nothing, even if all this plant were dispersed like leaves struck by the autumn wind; if, despite all these things, the ideal of love and service of God and his Blessed Mother were to grow in our hearts, then, my little children, we can say we are in full progress."

Thus Maximilian established priorities for his friars. Prayer came before work. Despite the stupendous activity of the city, he insisted that the friars spend three and a half hours each day in community prayer and meditation. The friars together shared the common life; there was no distinction between priest and brother. The only exception to the common poverty was those who were ill. Father Kolbe showered upon the sick the best of food and medicines.

*   *   *   *   *

Kolbe's story now takes an incredible turn. One day, when riding a train, Father Maximilian met some young Japanese students. He was moved by their kindliness and courtesy. His heart was broken to know that these fine young people were deprived of the knowledge of Christ and his Gospel. Characteristically, he felt he had to do something. Thus Maximilian approached his superiors to seek permission to establish a City of the Immaculate in Japan.

From anybody else the idea would have been bizarre. After two decades, however, Father Kolbe's superiors had learned to expect anything of him.

Thus in February, 1930, along with four brothers, Maximilian left the City of the Immaculate in Poland to establish another such community in far-off Japan. With characteristic humility, Maximilian slipped quietly out of Poland. He took leave of neither his brother, a Franciscan priest, nor his mother, who by now was with the sisters in Cracow. In the tenderness of his own heart he could not bear such farewells. He wrote later from Japan to his mother: "You will forgive me, Mother, for not calling on you before going on my journey."

As the little group made its way through Europe to the port of Marseilles, France, Maximilian stopped at Lisieux, the burial place of St. Therese. He also visited Lourdes.

The missionary spirit of Therese of Lisieux who, from her hidden cell, prayed to conquer the whole world, appealed to Maximilian's belief that the life of prayer and personal holiness had to be the basis for any work for Christ and his Mother.

In May, 1930, the little band of friars arrived at Nagasaki, Japan. The Japanese bishop, delighted with Father Maximilian's plans, offered his

Father Kolbe, with glasses, chats with
Prince Drucki-Lubecki. In 1927 the prince gave the friars a large
tract of land outside Warsaw where they constructed the City of the Immaculate.

Within a decade after beginning the City of the Immaculate,
over 700 brothers joined him in his publications work.

support immediately. In return, the prelate requested that the priest teach
philosophy and theology in the Nagasaki seminary. The friar joyfully acceded
and the first steps toward building a Japanese City of the Immaculate were
taken.

These Polish friars were either full of madness or full of faith. About
to publish a magazine in Japanese, they could neither read, write, nor speak
Japanese. They knew nothing of Japanese law, culture, labor practices, or
machinery. In short, they knew nothing of Japan. Yet, incredibly, within
one month, Father Maximilian and his group published and distributed their
first Japanese issue of *The Knight*.

The minor miracle was the work of many hands and minds. A Japanese Methodist translated Italian and English articles into Japanese, and a
Japanese university professor translated articles from German into Japanese

for this first issue. Father Maximilian wrote articles in Latin, and a Japanese seminarian translated the Latin into Japanese. Thus final articles often went from Polish, to Latin, to Japanese. Only Mary prevented this first issue of *The Knight* from collapsing like the Tower of Babel.

To further comprehend the impossible task these men brought off, it was absolutely contrary to Japanese custom and etiquette to seek subscriptions through the mail. Thus the friars advertised *The Knight* in trains, streets, and other public places. Interested Japanese would send a postcard with their address. On receipt of this, and only on receipt of that card, could the friars solicit a subscription to their magazine.

The very simplicity and courage of these friars attracted both Christian and non-Christian Japanese. Vocations began to come to the Franciscans from the people about them. Within four years the little community of five had grown to twenty-four friars. Maximilian soon established a seminary, and within six years there were some 20 Japanese studying for the priesthood in the Franciscan Order.

Friars called their Japanese foundation "The Garden of Mary Immaculate." Years later, in 1945, the Garden was miraculously untouched in the atomic bombing of Nagasaki. Immediately following the atomic bombing, the city swarmed with frightened and abandoned children. The Franciscan friars accepted as many of these tiny victims of war as they could into the Garden of the Immaculate, and soon an orphanage was established and in time contained one thousand children.

His superiors summoned Father Maximilian to come to Poland for the 1936 general meeting of their community. Kolbe returned to his native land, delighted with the progress in Japan, hopeful of establishing a similar operation in India, and happy to revisit the City of the Immaculate in his beloved Niepokalanow.

All, however, was not well. Father Maximilian's physical disabilities were mounting. His health had taken an inevitable downward course. Frequent hemorrhaging and discharges of blood indicated a dangerous condition.

Because of his health, his provincial superiors insisted that Father Kolbe remain in Poland at the City of the Immaculate. He willingly accepted this assignment. The friars there looked to him for the spiritual leadership they had so sorely missed during his years in Japan. They delighted in calling him "Father." He would respond: "I am your father, even more so than your earthly father from whom you have received your physical life. Through me, you have received a spiritual life, and this is a divine life; through me, you have received your religious vocation, which is more than physical life." To this day, men who knew him recall his spirit of intense kindness, gentleness, and paternal love.

One quiet evening, while sitting with a group of friars after dinner, he said: "My dear sons, if only you knew how happy I am. My heart is over-flowing with happiness and peace. At the bottom of my heart an unspeakable calm reigns." Father Maximilian continued: "My dear sons, love the Im-maculate. Love her and she will make you happy. Trust her without limits. Not all can understand Mary. This understanding can be gained only by prayer." Then the priest paused and haltingly added: "I have something else to tell you, but perhaps this is enough."

The friars pressed him to go on. "All right, I will tell you. The reason that I am very happy and filled with joy is that I have been given an assurance of heaven."

Those who heard him make this statement remember to this day how his voice shook. A moment of complete silence followed. Then Father Maximilian seemed to be ready to say something else.

The friars pressed him for more information. Acknowledging he had received this assurance of heaven in Japan, he continued: "I have revealed this secret to you to strengthen your courage and spiritual energies for the difficulties ahead. There will be trials, temptations and discouragements. The memory of tonight will strengthen you and help you to persevere in your religious life. It will strengthen you for the sacrifice which Mary will ask of you.

"Love the Immaculate," he pleaded; "love the Immaculate." He begged the friars not to tell anyone of this extraordinary conversation until after his death. He reiterated with sorrow that only because the terrible trial was near did he tell them of Mary's promise.

On September 1, 1939, Hitler hurled his armies into Poland and World War II, the worst cataclysm mankind has ever known, was thus launched. Within weeks, German armies, superior in numbers and equipment, overran Poland. Russians moved against Poland from the east.

Father Kolbe was under no illusions about the treatment he would receive at Nazi hands. He had condemned in his press and on his radio station the doctrines of both Nazism and Communism. The friar frequently referred to the suffering that these godless philosophies would ultimately bring upon the world.

Furthermore, Kolbe, in the last days of August, 1939, spoke to his Franciscan confreres regarding his own life. He described the three stages of his life to his Franciscan brethren.

The first stage he described as a preparation for his apostolic activities; the second stage as the actual apostolate. There would finally be the stage of suffering.

Nazis escort Father Kolbe and his fellow Franciscans
to prison, the first step in their own cruel Way of the Cross.

"The third stage of my life," he stated, "will be my lot shortly. It will be one of suffering. But by whom, where, how, and in what form this suffering will come, is known only to the Immaculate Mother. I would like to suffer and die in a knightly manner, even to the shedding of the last drop of my blood, to hasten the day of gaining the whole world for the Immaculate Mother of God."

The Nazis would soon oblige him.

After the Nazis quickly overran Poland, Maximilian and some of his friars at the City of the Immaculate were put into jail. Soon afterwards they were released, and by December 8, 1939, Maximilian had returned to Niepokalanow. The Nazis had occupied the place and established a concentration camp there. But they permitted Father Kolbe and a few of his friars to live there. In 1940 Maximilian actually received permission to resume his printing of *The Knight*. And on December 8, 1940, he managed to publish what turned out to be the last issue of his beloved magazine.

The Gestapo, however, were watching Kolbe as a snake watches its prey. Finally they struck, and in February, 1941, they arrested the priest. He was jailed just outside Warsaw.

On May 28, 1941, Father Kolbe, suffering again from tubercular attacks, joined a transport of 320 prisoners to Auschwitz. At Auschwitz, jailers gave him identification number 16670, and first assigned him to block 17. Nazi guards forced the seriously ill priest to haul heavy carts of gravel for the construction of the crematorium walls. Despite beatings and unbelievable indignities, the jailers were unable to break down Father Maximilian's calmness and gentleness. A fellow prisoner recalls the priest encouraging the inmates. "No, no," the little friar would say, "these Nazis will not kill our souls, since we prisoners certainly distinguish ourselves quite definitely from our tormentors; they will not be able to deprive us of the dignity of our Catholic belief. We will not give up. And when we die, then we die pure and peaceful, resigned to God in our hearts."

A source of spiritual strength to all about him, the little priest frustrated Nazi attempts to reduce these Poles and European Jews into groveling animals. Jailers reserved the dirtiest jobs for him and cursed and ridiculed him because of his priesthood. From time to time, they would set dogs on

The ovens at Auschwitz, part of "the final solution" that claimed the lives of millions of Jews and Christians during World War II.

him, force him to carry corpses to the crematorium, and beat him unmercifully. Eventually poor Maximilian collapsed with total exhaustion and was hospitalized.

Father Conrad Szweda, a fellow captive, writes:

Father Kolbe's face was lined with scars, his eyes lifeless; the fever burned in his body so that his mouth dried out; he could no longer speak. But all were impressed by his manliness and resignation with which he bore his sufferings. Often he said: "For Jesus Christ, I am prepared to suffer still more." Even though suffering intense pain, Maximilian heard the confessions of others, prayed with them, and often gave them little conferences on Mary. He was a priest every inch of his burned-out body.

By the very power of his presence, Kolbe managed to rescue these poor, beaten people from the degradation that threatened them, and somehow kept them living on a human level. Doctor Joseph Stemler, another prisoner, remembers:

> Like many others, I crawled at night in the infirmary on the bare floor to the bed of Father Maximilian. The greeting was moving. We exchanged some impressions on the frightful crematorium. He encouraged me, and I confessed. Discouragement and doubt threatened to overwhelm me; but I still wanted to love. He helped me to strengthen my belief in the final victory of good. "Hatred is not creative," he whispered to me. "Our sorrow is necessary that those who live after us may be happy." His reflections on the mercy of God went straight to my heart. His words to forgive the persecutors, and to overcome evil with good, kept me from collapsing into despair.

A Protestant doctor writes of Kolbe that:

> . . . although tuberculosis consumed him, he remained calm . . . ; through his living belief in God and his providence, with his unshakable hope and, before all else, in his love of God and neighbor, he distinguished himself from all. Although I was in Auschwitz from 1941 until 1945, I knew of no other similar case of such heroic love of neighbor.

It was this indomitable man who entered the Nazi death bunker with nine other prisoners in July, 1941.

Bruno Burgowiec remembers his daily contacts with the men in Maximilian's bunker. "So desperate did their situation become," he states, "that they were forced to drink their own urine. Father Maximilian did not whine, neither did he murmur. He encouraged and comforted the others."

To the end of his long, harrowing suffering, Maximilian could amaze his captors. Indeed, the final victory was to be his. One cannot help but think of Christ emerging from his tomb to bring new life to men. Kolbe indeed in death outwitted all the evil forces of violence of World War II.

Stefan Cardinal Wyszynski, Primate of Poland, spoke of him as the man who really won the war.

When questioned by the Gestapo commandant as to why he wanted to take Sergeant Gajowniczek's place, Kolbe cited only one reason. "I am," he said, "a Catholic priest." Pope Paul called this Father Maximilian's "incomparable answer."

5. Teresa of Calcutta

Agnes Boyaxhiu was born of Albanian parents at Skopje, Yugoslavia, on August 27, 1910. As a young girl she attended the government schools in Yugoslavia along with her brother and sister. Her family was of peasant stock. Her education therefore included more than just attending school. She worked in the fields and absorbed the characteristics of patience and down-to-earthness, the capacity for hard work, and the acceptance of inevitable obstacles in life. These helped the young girl to learn that quick solutions are usually no solutions to the problems of life.

Agnes' parents were Catholic: she accepted the tenets and beliefs of the faith with simplicity and directness. Her faith was as real to her as the earth she farmed and the people with whom she studied and grew up. During the course of her schooling she joined the Sodality of the Blessed Virgin Mary. This was nothing exceptional; most of the young girls of her village did the same thing. Her home was a happy one. She grew up in an atmosphere of love, contentment and peace.

While still in her teens she began to desire to serve God. It happened that some Jesuit priests who were directors of the Sodality had left to do missionary work in India. She became interested and attracted to this

119

type of work and volunteered to go to India to serve the people there. The Jesuits put her in touch with the Loretto nuns in Ireland, who had missions in Calcutta. Young Agnes corresponded with the Loretto nuns and eventually was accepted by them.

In later life, when asked about her choice of vocation, she remarked that once she had entered the religious life, she never felt any urge to leave it. Making the decision, however, "was not easy."

"Between 12 and 18," she remarked, "I did not want to become a nun. We were a very happy family. But when I was 18, I decided to leave my home and become a nun. Since then, more than forty years, I never doubted, even for a second, that I had done the right thing. It was the will of God; it was his choice."

In 1928 young Agnes went to Ireland to begin her religious career. She cast her lot with the Lord completely and without qualification. She was happy from the first moments of her contact with the Sisters of Loretto. She was initiated into the religious life and Loretto Abbey, Rathfarnham, Dublin, on November 29, 1928. Very soon after her reception into the convent, the young novice experienced what was later to become the pattern of her life. Her "home" was not to be rooted in any one particular place. She would follow the Spirit of God wherever it led her. Her superiors almost immediately sent her from Ireland to India to begin her novitiate and, in 1929, her teaching career.

She returned to Ireland in 1931 and made her simple vows of poverty, chastity, and obedience. For some 20 years she was a member of the Sisters of Loretto. She remembers this religious community with tenderness, love, and joy. The training that she received among them helped her to form and shape her life. This attitude of deep faith and commitment and willingness to follow God wherever he would lead her stood her in good stead as the mission of her life gradually unfolded.

*   *   *   *   *

In 1929, young Sister Teresa was appointed to St. Mary's High School in Calcutta, where she taught geography. She was very popular as a teacher and also manifested genuine talent as an administrator. For some years she was principal at St. Mary's. She was also responsible for the Daughters of St. Anne, an Indian religious Order attached to the Loretto Sisters. Her natural friendliness drew many of her young girl students to her.

In her discussions with them she often spoke of the poor and of Christian responsibility to them. These girls were of mixed religious backgrounds. Socially, most of them were from the middle class, but some were from the highest and wealthiest class of Indians.

They were very attracted to Sister Teresa, to her natural qualities, her vibrant and strong, quiet, calm personality. From time to time they would discuss Christianity and the need of service to the poor. It was difficult for the girls, products of Indian society, to comprehend the teachings of Christ regarding love for the poor. The poor were so much with them that they were commonplace, an accepted fact of life. Thousands, literally thousands of people, died of starvation every year on the streets of Calcutta. The only way one could possibly survive in the face of such misery was to ignore it. There seemed to be no way of overcoming or handling what always has been, and still is, a dreadful and seemingly insoluble problem in India.

The non-Christian Indian often comes to terms with the problem by saying that the poor are suffering for their sins. Other Indians who believe in reincarnation hold that the poor live this miserable existence because of some sins they have committed in a previous existence. They hope that the

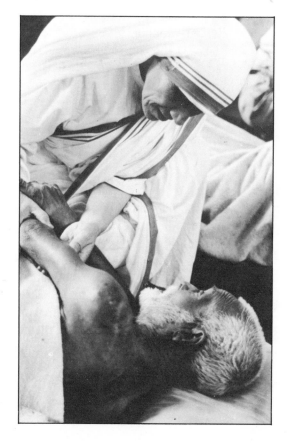

The sisters work with the poorest of the poor in Calcutta.

poor will purify their souls through suffering and, after their merciful release in death, will enter a new existence that will be more pleasant. Others, of course, simply do not care. There is a further group who dare not care because of the magnitude of the problem.

Sister Teresa's young pupils were made aware of the problem and discussed it with her. She was very happy teaching, but God was to lead her from the classroom and the great vocation of teaching to another classroom as wide as the world and crammed with pupils who hungered and thirsted from a different type of need. It all happened when Sister Teresa was on her way to her annual retreat in 1946.

"The Spirit of God," Scripture tells us, "breathes where he wills." The Spirit of God touched the heart of this sister as she sat on a little train that was huffing and puffing its way up to the tea country of Darjeeling. Sister was looking forward to the peace and rest of the annual retreat. While she sat watching the countryside roll by the train window, as she said later, "I heard the call to give up all and follow him into the slums to serve among the poorest of the poor." It is impossible to describe the movement of God within the human heart. The only term we can use, and the only term Sister Teresa could use, was the word "called." But it was a call as old as that of Abraham to leave his father's house. She was asked to leave her own religious community and enter the strange and frightening world of India's poor.

The call of God caused her some anguish. She was at home at St. Mary's school and convent with its pleasant garden, eager schoolgirls, congenial colleagues, and rewarding work. And just as she had difficulty in leaving her childhood home to answer God's call to the religious life, so now she had to experience a new tearing from a peaceful, happy, and joyous relationship that she had built up during 20 years in India.

The tenth of September, 1946, was a day of decision. She requested permission to live alone outside the cloister. The Mother General of the Loretto nuns gave her permission to write to Rome. Because she had taken her final vows, the procedures of canon law, at least in those days, were rather lengthy. In her letter she simply stated that she felt she had a vocation and that God was calling her to give up all and to surrender herself to him in the service of the poorest of the poor in the slums of Calcutta. Her request,

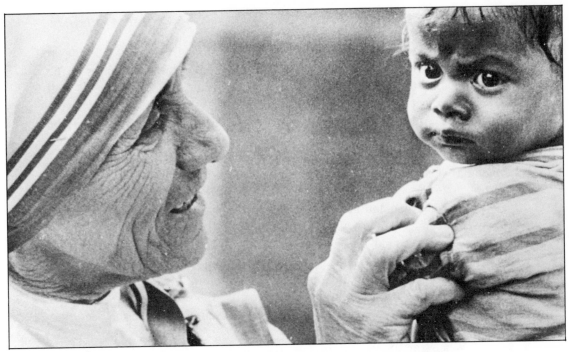

Mother Teresa holds a youngster after a cyclone ravaged the state of Andhra Pradesh.

taken to Rome, was eventually approved.

After permission came, Sister Teresa, on August 8, 1948, left the lovely calm of the Loretto convent and put aside the religious habit she had worn for so many years, and walked out into the terribly noisy streets of Calcutta. She was to lead the life of a religious, but under obedience to the Archbishop of Calcutta. It was a tremendous sacrifice for her. It was the first bitter step in the journey God was asking her to undertake.

She left the convent with a few Indian rupees in her pocket, and made her way to the poorest and most wretched parts of the city and found lodging there. (A rupee is about fourteen cents!)

To symbolize her new life-style and mission, Sister Teresa had laid aside her religious habit and clothed herself in a white Indian sari with a blue border.

Sister went to the American Medical Missionary Sisters in Patna to get a little training in medical work, so that she could enter the houses of the poor and minister to the physical needs of the many who were ill, as well as work as a teacher.

The American Medical Missionary Sisters trained her well in the rudiments of medical care. She returned to Calcutta and at first lived with the Little Sisters of the Poor. Eventually she moved into a compound belonging to a family in the slums. Her total capital, at this point, was five rupees!

The courage and audacity of this lady boggle the imagination. Facing the overwhelming misery of Calcutta, she began her task believing that a journey of a thousand miles begins with the first step—that it is better to light one candle than to curse the darkness. She did both of these things by opening a tiny school on the first day of her new mission. She had five children present in the classroom, and shortly after that she had more and more children. Looking back now over more than 30 years, she sees that the school is still going.

When questioned about her audacity, she smiles calmly, and with extreme good humor answers: "I was so sure then, and I am still convinced that it is God, not I, doing this work. I wasn't afraid then. I knew that if the work was mine it would die with me. I knew it was his work and that it will live and bring much good."

As a teacher her first pupils were older children. She began teaching them the alphabet, because they had never been to school—no school wanted them—and basic lessons in hygiene such as how to wash themselves.

Her former pupils at St. Mary's School were not unfamiliar with Sister Teresa's new mission, and soon after she opened the school for the poor, two or three girls came from St. Mary's to help her with the children. Gradually the work grew, and some ladies from Calcutta who had been teachers also came to help. Gradually, too, people came to know what she was doing, and they brought her food, clothing, and money. She never asked for money, and she always felt that whatever she received came from God's hands. She wanted to serve the poor purely for love of God, and she was soon to find out that God was going to bless her in ways she had never dreamed.

In 1949, one of her former pupils, Shubashini Das, a Bengali, came to her and said that she wanted to become a religious and work with Sister Teresa as a nun. Now called Sister Agnes, Shubashini was the first of 10 former pupils who soon came to Sister Teresa. "One by one," she said, "the girls surrendered themselves to God to serve the poorest of the poor, to give their all to God." This little group of 10 became the nucleus of dedicated women who would be called the Missionaries of Charity. Other helpers came: doctors and nurses came to help on a voluntary basis. In 1952 Sister (now Mother) Teresa took another most significant step: she opened her first home for the dying to care for the people who had been abandoned by their families and left to die on the streets.

As the years went by, she began to attract vocations from all over India to her work. Her greatest influence was to make the Indians themselves face the basic need to understand the sufferings of the poor.

Malcolm Muggeridge, the English television personality, writes:

> I should never have believed it possible, knowing India as I do
> over a number of years, to induce Indian girls of good family
> to tend to outcasts and untouchables brought in from the Cal-
> cutta streets. Yet this, precisely, is the very first task that
> Mother Teresa gives her postulants to do. They do it, not just
> in obedience, but cheerfully and ardently, and gather around
> her in even greater numbers for the privilege of doing it.

Thus Mother Teresa chose to live in the slums of Calcutta; amid all the dirt and disease and dying she radiated a spirit so indomitable, a faith so strong, a love so abounding, that they cleansed and brought life to all about her.

Pope Paul VI, in speaking of this woman, said:

> We discover a law: that good multiplies itself. The work of
> Mother Teresa shows this. Her inexhaustible energy, her po-
> tential for good, the resource of her human heart, are poured
> out. The leaven of her personal sacrifice as well as her courage
> made her do unbelievable things with God's help.

The Pope went on to say that when good demands to express itself, the means to do so will always be found. "The one who wishes to do good will always find a way to do it. . . . The needs of others often become a challenge to the one who has the genius for doing good and the gift of love." Indeed the need that Mother Teresa was now to uncover could hardly be more real and more overwhelming. And she would be almost completely inadequate to take care of it.

But she was the type of woman who had to respond to the imperative of need. She saw a life of personal poverty as a necessary condition for the work she was about to undertake. And she undertook this work with great cheer and joy because she knew that while she could never see its full value here in this world, by doing God's work she would someday see in heaven the results of his work and she would come to love God more because of the very people she was helping.

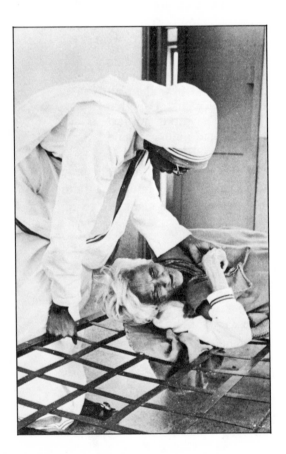

And this is another characteristic which now definitely began to manifest itself. The way she describes it is: "The poor deserve not just service and dedication, but also the joy that belongs to human love." Never did anyone need human love more than these people who were to become the objects of her love.

One day, while on the streets of Calcutta, she saw a dying lady who had been half eaten by rats and ants. She picked her up, brought her to a hospital, but the hospital could not do anything for the lady. Undaunted, Mother Teresa took the poor woman to the city hall and asked the authorities to give her a place where she could bring these dying people who filled the streets.

A woman, physically and mentally ill, in the home for the dying destitutes in New Delhi has no mattress on her bed. It was taken from her when she began to eat it.

The city health officer took Mother to an abandoned Kali temple which had within it a pagan caravansary or hostel. In former times, Hindus would worship Kali, the goddess of death, one of the most frightening of Hindu deities, usually done in preparation for burying their own dead. The dead would then be removed to the riverbank and burned on a fiery pyre. Those who had performed the last rites for their dead would then return to the Kali temple to rest.

The health officer asked Sister if she would accept the empty Kali temple. She says, "I was very happy to have that place for many reasons, but especially knowing that it was the center of worship and devotion of the Hindus."

Within 24 hours she had patients in there, and she started the work of the home for the sick and destitute dying. Since that day the sisters have picked up thousands of people from the streets, many of whom have lived as the result of their care. Mother and the sisters would also attempt to obtain decent employment for those they had revived.

One might reasonably ask why Mother would be concerned about the dying? She knew that the only comfort she could provide for them in their last hours was to show them that there were some people who really did love them, who really wanted them; and at least for the few hours that they had to live, they would know divine and human love. Mother Teresa lavished this love on the poorest of the poor as a final reminder, as their days in this world ended, that they were indeed children of God and that they had not been forgotten by their fellow human beings.

The school continued to flourish, but Mother Teresa now moved into caring for the sick and dying. The sisters who at first used to pick up the dead and the dying in the streets and bring them to the Kali temple soon became so well known that they no longer had to perform this task. The Indian people themselves began to get involved. They would bring the dying from the streets to the sisters. The sisters themselves could remain to comfort, wash, clothe, and give what little medicines they had to those who were dying.

A reporter from the *Canadian Register,* describing the Home for the Dying, writes: "When you stand by the temple of Kali in Calcutta, death is very close. The temple is dedicated to the most frightening of the Hindu deities. . . . Nearby, the burning ghats, on the banks of the Hooghly River, consume the bodies of Calcutta's dead. And a few steps away stands the Home for Dying Destitutes."

As the work grew, Mother Teresa divided the two floors of the temple, the lower for the men, the upper for the women. The people who are brought in are in the last gasp of life—really the living dead. But the amazing thing is that the love that Mother and her sisters lavish on these people very often brings them back to life.

"The most prevalent disease today," Mother Teresa has said, "is not leprosy or tuberculosis, but rather the feeling of being unwanted, uncared for, deserted by everybody. Today people are falling to this side or that side of the road," she explains. "The aim of our Society is to satiate the thirst of Jesus. We do this through living the poverty of Christ. We love him in this distressing disguise."

In the years following the Pakistani war, the refugee problem added to the depressing human misery in India. Mother Teresa, the angel of the slums, continued to accept all the victims, not only of poverty but of war.

The municipal hospitals would not accept the dying people of the streets, but the municipal ambulances, contrary to their previous custom, began to pick up these people and to bring them to the sisters in their converted temple. In short, the Home for the Dying became the last refuge for the street cases that no hospital wanted, or for people who had absolutely no one to take care of them.

One would think that trying to care for the destitute dying on the streets of Calcutta would be enough for any woman and any religious order. But it is not so with Mother Teresa. Her love is so generous and so all-embracing that it soon became evident to her that, besides the children and the dying on the streets, there were the lepers. She started to gather them, back in 1957, when five lepers came to the home for the destitute and dying because they had lost their jobs. They had no shelter and no place to go.

As usual, Mother Teresa accepted them and did her best, and before long, an Indian doctor, a specialist in leprosy care, joined her and began training the sisters for service to the lepers.

The leper, although he may have been well-educated, rich, and a capable person, is separated from Indian society and thrown out of his home for fear that the disease will be contracted by the rest of the family. Very often, their own children do not want to see the lepers anymore.

"We have among our lepers here in Calcutta," Mother says, "very high positions in life. But, owing to the disease, they are now living in the slums, unknown, unloved, and uncared for." It matters not what faith the sufferer professes. All suffering human beings—Hindu, Mohammedan, and those of the numberless sectaries—are admitted; they are all Christ in disguise.

Mother Teresa had her sisters specially trained in modern techniques of treating lepers; and with the assistance of new drugs and medicines, the sisters are able to stem the awful disease if the lepers seek help in time. Presently there are nearly 10,000 lepers in Calcutta under the care of the sisters.

For those past curing, Mother has built a "Town of Peace" on land that the Indian government has donated to her. The complex includes community kitchens, gardens, workshops, school, dispensary, and poultry farm. The lepers, instead of sitting around and waiting for the disease to claim them, are trained in light industries and taught how to make firebricks for neighboring factories.

One would wonder about the practicality of all this, but those who have visited the Shanti Nagar (Town of Peace) report that the project is moving along very well and that the lepers are happy and are working. Indeed, they are even running a printing press with their broken stumps for hands.

Mother Teresa's background has helped her to be a very practical planner and organizer. She is a very good businesswoman and manages somehow to disarm and draw the best out of the people with whom she deals in the business world. They admire her good business sense. With all she has to manage, this, too, is a heavenly gift.

Her whole purpose in establishing these small industries is to train the lepers whose disease may be arrested, so that they will be able to return and live an ordinary citizen's life at home when their health has been restored. This will help them avoid becoming common beggars.

This underlines another deep feeling surrounding Mother Teresa's work: her intense respect for the dignity of each individual person with whom she comes into contact.

Pope Paul has said that good tends to multiply itself. So it has been with all of Mother Teresa's work. She soon found herself involved in establishing homes for crippled and unwanted children in Calcutta and opening other schools. Mother has also developed a fleet of mobile clinics for treating lepers and those with other kinds of illnesses. In short, her work just seemed to grow by leaps and bounds. But if it is true that God makes demands of those who serve him, then he certainly helps them find the means to fulfill these demands.

*   *   *   *   *

The vocations to Mother's little order steadily increased. In 1950, Pope Pius XII made the community a diocesan congregation, and in 1965 it became a pontifical group. In 1950 there were only 12 members of the Missionaries of Charity. During the next decade in Calcutta the sisters trained diligently for the various types of work ahead of them. In 1959 they opened their first house in Dranchi; a little later another house in Delhi, India. The number of sisters began to increase very, very rapidly. They came mostly from the middle class; some from the richer and higher class. There are a number of Anglo-Indian girls who have joined the congregation, most of whom are very well-educated.

The sisters are well-trained. "From the day they join the community, we spend a good deal of time in training our sisters," Mother says, "especially in the spirit and life of our Society. . . . Along with the spiritual training, the young aspirants have to go to the slums. This is part of their novitiate training." Familiarity with the poor is in preparation for the fourth vow the sisters take, along with the usual three vows of poverty, chastity and obedience; and that is to give wholehearted, free service to the poor and suffering. In a time when religious congregations are experiencing a great deal of difficulty, both in attracting members and suffering many losses, this new congregation, the Missionaries of Charity, is growing by leaps and bounds. There is no doubt that it is in response to the very real needs of

The home for the dying destitutes maintained by the Missionaries of Charity for the poor of New Delhi.

the people that they are increasing in numbers.

There is also another characteristic of the sisters that seems to strike everyone who comes into contact with them, and that is the spirit of joy that they radiate. The spirit of their congregation is not simply to carry on useful and necessary work to heal and educate, and to feed and comfort the suffering, but, rather, to do all of this in a spirit of happiness and joy.

Mother Teresa notes: "We want our poor to feel that they are loved. If we went to them with a sad face, we would only make them more depressed." After more than 30 years of work among the people, the sisters know that medicine for leprosy has been found and that the disease can be arrested. There is medicine for tuberculosis, and consumptives can be cured. As Mother goes on to say, "For all kinds of diseases there are medicines and cures. But for the disease of being unwanted, except where there are willing hands to serve and there is a loving heart to love, I don't think this terrible disease can ever be cured. The poor little children from the streets of Calcutta, some of them abandoned by their parents, some left in hospitals, some brought in from jail—all somehow manage to make their way to Mother Teresa. The sisters always can find one more bed for one more child.

Aware that there are those who cry that there are too many children in India and who would think it a mercy if many of them died, Mother, the total realist, says: "I do not agree with people who say there are too many children in India. God provides for the flowers and the birds, for everything in the world that he has created. And those little children are his life. There can never be enough."

Shortly after the approval in 1950 of the Missionaries of Charity, the movement initiated by Mother Teresa began to expand beyond the boundaries of Calcutta and into the Indian countryside. Within short order the sisters were found throughout India, as Mother Teresa traveled the immense distances of that country, establishing institutions all over it.

Today there are some 30 houses in India, where more than 600 Missionaries of Charity devote themselves to various works for the poor. Of course, most of these religious are Indian ladies. A group of men, inspired by the work of Mother Teresa, established an Order of Missionary Brothers of Charity in 1963. They currently have a foundation in Los Angeles.

"We felt a need for men who would take care of the boys in the schools and the men in the Home for the Dying," explains Mother Teresa. The brothers, numbering over 100, do exactly the same kind of work as the sisters, and live the same type of life. They are much better able to assist in certain areas with both the ill and the aged men and in the schools and orphanages for male students.

From the very first, the magic of Mother Teresa's mission attracted people from all over Calcutta. Hindus, Mohammedans, and Christians donated their time, their talent, and their money to furthering the enormous work of charity of the sisters. Some of them even more closely identified themselves with Mother Teresa and her religious by becoming affiliated. These are called Co-Workers, and in 1969 the constitution of their associa-

The Missionaries of Charity aided the residents of Andhra Pradesh
where an estimated 25,000 died in a cyclone in 1977.

tion was presented to Pope Paul VI and received his blessing.

Malcolm Muggeridge notes, "When the rich come to Mother Teresa,
they are liable to leave a little less rich, which she considers is conferring a
great favor on them." Mother Teresa has never accepted any government
grants in connection with her medical and social work because it would
involve keeping accounts. She does her best to keep any kind of administrative work to a minimum. At times, two nuns with one typewriter between
them handle the administration of the entire organization.

One of her best-known benefactors has been Pope Paul VI. When
he visited India he presented her with his white ceremonial motor car. Mother
Teresa never even set foot in it, and immediately put it up for raffle and
raised $98,000 to get her leper colony started.

Mother Teresa aims to directly involve anyone who wants to help her with the poor. If a doctor wants to help, she prefers that he treat the ill rather than give her money. Any professional skill is immediately put to work directly in connection with the poor. She finds that in doing this, the person or benefactor begins to overcome his initial fear of, and sometimes revulsion to, the world of the poor, and finds in the poor a source of real life and joy. What happens then is that the person who begins to serve the poor finds that he or she is engaged in a real brotherly effort to make life better both for the person who is served and the person serving.

One of Mother Teresa's great admirers, a lay person, describes his reaction in the following words:

> I found I went through three phases when I visited the Home for the Dying, the lepers, and the unwanted children. The first was horror mixed with pity; the second, compassion pure and simple; and the third, reaching far beyond compassion—something I had never experienced before—an awareness that these dying and derelict men and women, these lepers with stumps instead of hands, these unwanted children, were not pitiable, repulsive, or forlorn, but, rather, dear and delightful; as it might be, friends of long standing, brothers and sisters.

Thus Mother Teresa managed to reveal to those who work with her the very heart and mystery of the Christian faith.

Mother Teresa has said that her work and that of all her religious and Co-Workers can only be fruitful and beautiful if it is built on faith. "Faith in Christ, who has said, 'I was hungry, . . . I was naked, . . . I was sick, . . . I was homeless, and you did this for me.' On these words of Christ, all of our work is based," Mother comments. She teaches that love, to be true, has to be a giving love. In her view, love and faith in Christ go together and complete each other. People find this source of life and joy by getting in touch with those who are in need. For it is in people that we find God.

In speaking of her Co-Workers, she says:

> I want them to give their hands to serve the people and their hearts to love the people. For, unless they come into very close contact with the poor, it is very difficult for them to know who the poor are. That is why, here in Calcutta, we have many non-Christians and Christians working together in the

Home for the Dying and in other places. We have groups who are preparing the medicine and bandages for the lepers. For example, an Australian came some time ago and explained that he wanted to give a big donation. But, after giving the donation, he said "That is something outside of me, but I want to give something of me." Now he comes regularly to the Home for the Dying, and he shaves the people and talks to them. He could have spent that time on himself, not just his money. He wanted to give something of himself, and he gives it.

Thus Mother Teresa always insists on her Co-Workers working for the people. She never requests money of them or asks anything from them. "I just ask them to come and love the people, to give their hands to serve them, and their hearts to love them."

Her experience has been that when the Co-Workers are in touch with the poor, their first impulse is to do something for them and then they become involved. "Once the Co-Workers realize how lovable these poor are, they do all they can to love and serve them."

Thus Mother Teresa has managed to transmit not only to her religious but to these Co-Workers of every faith her creed of service to the poor. It goes something like this:

> I do not agree with the big way of doing things. To us what matters is an individual. To get to love the person, we must come into closer contact with him. If we wait till we get a big operation, then we will be lost in the numbers. We will never be able to show that love and respect for the person.

*   *   *   *   *

Beginning in 1965, the Missionaries of Charity began to move outside of India also. Quickly the sisters responded to needs wherever manifested—places like Venezuela, Sri Lanka, and Tanzania. In Rome, at the special request of the Holy Father, the sisters opened up a center in the slums of the city. In Australia the Aborigines needed help, and the sisters opened up a center in Bourke. In Melbourne there was a need on the docks and waterfronts, so the sisters went there. In Amman, Jordan, there was a need

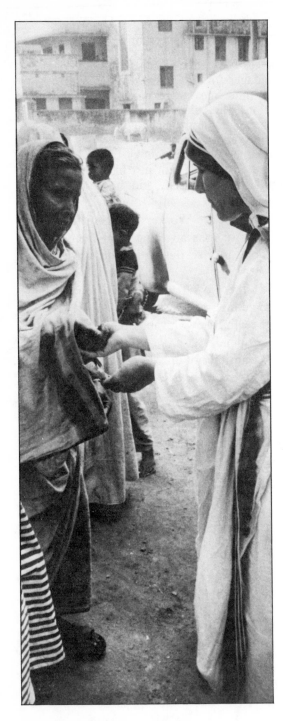

to relieve the suffering and pain among the refugees, and the sisters opened up a center. Co-Workers are gathering and clustering about the sisters at all of these foundations. There are two foundations of the sisters in New York City, South Bronx. One, a convent dedicated to the active apostolate, and the other, to the contemplative life.

The life of these sisters is rugged and austere by worldly standards. Yet everyone who comes into contact with them notes their happiness and the atmosphere of joy. Indeed, the term "luminosity" is used to describe them. This is an external, glowing quality that radiates from an interior fire of the spirit.

Mother Teresa says, "The poor deserve not just service and dedication, but also the joy that belongs to human love." And this is why she attaches so much importance to developing, on a firm foundation, a spirit of joy.

The Co-Workers come from some unpredictable sources. Of course, there have been Hindu and Moslem doctors and dentists and other professional people, as well as Protestants, Catholics, and Jews. Some of the more touching Co-Workers are among the school children of Europe. The little

The Missionaries distribute medicine to the poor of India.

children of England are donating
enough money to help provide bread
for thousands of children in India. The
children of Denmark are making sacrifices to give a glass of milk each day.
The children in Germany are making
sacrifices to give one multivitamin cap-
sule daily. Mother sees these as ways
to greater love and hope for our Western world. There are those who maintain there is such an atmosphere of
selfishness and overwhelming distrust
and fear in the Western world that we
will never be able to revive the spirit
of faith and love among nations.
Mother Teresa has no such pessimistic
feelings.

She sees, as one of the greatest
evils of our times, the fact the majority
of individuals in the more advanced
and wealthy societies are so caught up
in the rush of life that they lose interest
in everything outside themselves, in-
cluding suffering, which is far away
and out of sight. She even has concern
for the people in these wealthy societies
who are so caught up in this rush
that they fall down and are destroyed
by the very civilization which they
serve. They, too, should be the object
of compassion. She would like to love

*"Dearest Lord, may I see you today
and every day in the person of your sick,
and, while nursing them, may I minister
unto you."* Mother Teresa.

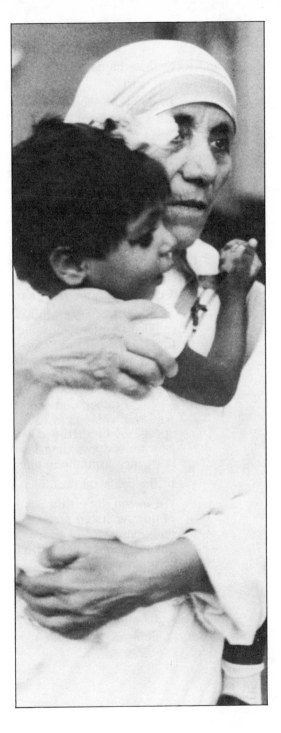

and serve these casualties of our civilization, for she reaches out to suffering wherever it exists.

In 1971 Mother Teresa's work was recognized and honored both in Rome and in Washington, D.C. The story of each of these awards points out the need for all of us to have before us the example of one who is really living the Christian life and mission. There is a great passion in the world among apostolic hearts to find someone who is at least trying to follow Christ and to lead the way for our imitation. There follows a need to honor such a person. Certainly this is true of the award granted by Pope Paul VI to Mother Teresa in January, 1971. At that time she became the first recipient of the International Pope John XXIII Peace Prize. The prize was granted to her because of her inspired work, the example that she has given, and the influence of the initiative of her charity in a world that is ravished by so much hate and cruelty. On the occasion of granting her this prize, Pope Paul said:

> . . . humble Mother Teresa, in whom we like to see personified the thousands and thousands of people dedicated full time to the personal service of the most needy. She is an example and symbol of the discovery of that human dedication in which lies the secret of the world's peace. It is the discovery, ever up to date, that man is our brother.
>
> Brotherhood and peace are by nature synonymous. . . . And she who comes to us as the missionary of charity is the apostle of brotherhood and the messenger of peace. That is why we are awarding her the peace prize; and to those who share her aspirations and her labors we give our blessing."

In the conferral document Pope Paul said:

> We intend, by giving this honor to you, to honor the memory of our venerated predecessor, Pope John XXIII, to serve also the great cause of peace, and to encourage all those throughout the world who untiringly dedicate themselves to the relief of sufferings of body and soul.

Before the year was out, Mother Teresa was also invited to Washington, D.C., to accept an award given by the Joseph P. Kennedy Foundation. At this affair, conducted at the new John F. Kennedy Center in Washington, a film was screened, showing Mother Teresa feeding the lepers in

Calcutta. The impression that it made on the gathered notables was deep and profound. Mother herself, as usual, remained happy and delighted to be there, unmoved by all the glitter and splendor. Her desire was to get back as soon as possible to her needy ones in India.

Thus we come to the end of our journey with Mother Teresa. She is still very much alive and active in this world, and God only knows where this journey, which she started in Yugoslavia some 70 years ago, will end. But of this we can be sure: that it will be a journey of the gospel coming to life in our modern world.

6. St. Francis of Assisi

"I'm in the clothing business," Peter Bernardone would have said, had you asked. And he would have liked you to ask.

He would, in those days, have liked you to ask about his family, for he had an Italian's deep pride in his three children. He especially prized one son and had completely spoiled him. This was Francis, now in his early twenties and already doing well in the family enterprises.

Francis was a constant delight to his father. The youth knew how to live, what he wanted, and how to get it. Nature had endowed him with fairly good looks, a personality that attracted and held friends, and a flair for good-humored leadership. None of these qualities would hurt his business career.

But it was this son, his favorite, who broke Peter Bernardone's heart. The boy turned on his father, and in a nasty family row that eventually boiled over into a public scene, Francis walked out of his father's life, his business, and left the fire of his father's pride to die down to cold, bitter ashes.

Things like this happen in families, but never for quite the same reasons, nor with the same consequences as in the family of Peter Bernardone, resident and wealthy merchant of Assisi, Italy, in 1206.

141

One might trace the roots of the family discord and the consequent amazing events of Francis' life to his entry into military service when he was 20 years of age. Previous to this date (1202), the favored son gave little indication that he was to swerve so radically from the course which his parents had so fondly set for him. After his enlistment he fought bravely in one bloody battle, but his troop suffered defeat. Taken prisoner of war, he was held captive for several months, then released and sent home. His father and mother cried with joy, and made up to him for the long months of suffering by showering him with affection and, what was perhaps more important to him at the time, even more spending money.

But the months in the dungeon had done their evil work. Francis became so sick he almost died, and had to convalesce for a whole year. It was during this year that, perhaps for the first time in his young life, he did some serious thinking. He probed the age-old problems: What am I? Where do I come from? Where am I going? What is this world? What is love?

Francis was Italian, a born poet, and Catholic. His faith supplied him with crystal-clear answers to his questions. As an Italian, his soul moved naturally to deep affection, love, joy. And as a poet he could see right through to the awful ramifications of those answers. What he saw frightened him and, as many a man before him, he backed off.

His health restored, he reentered Assisi's social whirl. He drove himself into its very vortex, hoping that it would yield up to him once more the things that would make him happy.

One night he saw in a dream the house of his birth changed into a stately palace. The walls of the palace were hung with magnificent armory, banners, shields, swords—all the terrible trophies of medieval warfare. A voice, remarkably clear and coherent for a dream, explained that this was to be his palace, the gathering place for his knights. The arms were theirs—the banners, tokens of their innumerable conquests. To complete this wonderful vision, a beautiful bride awaited him.

Francis woke in a happy sweat. He knew now that he was destined for glory—the kind he thought he really wanted.

A few mornings later he left Assisi to go to Southern Italy to enlist. He got as far as Spoleto, a day's journey, bivouacked, slept, and dreamt.

Again he heard the voice of the great promise, but this time it asked questions: "Francis, who can do more for you, the servant or the master?" Francis, enjoying some sense of practical politics, answered: "Why, the master!" And now came the dialogue that changed the course of Francis' life, and in many ways, the course of human history. "Why, then," the voice exclaimed, "are you seeking the servant instead of the master, the vassal instead of the prince?"

Francis, recognizing the voice as that of Christ, suddenly grew weary of retreat.

"Lord," he asked tiredly, "what will You have me do?"

"Return home. Your vision will have its spiritual fulfillment through Me."

And so the warrior returned to Assisi. Although the young people of Assisi rejoiced at his return (he was their acknowledged ringleader), they soon sensed that the wild one had changed. Something was quite evidently troubling him. Shadows passed quickly across his bright face, and sometimes his smile would harden and his crackling eyes go dull. The young ones unflinchingly concluded that the inevitable had happened. Francis had

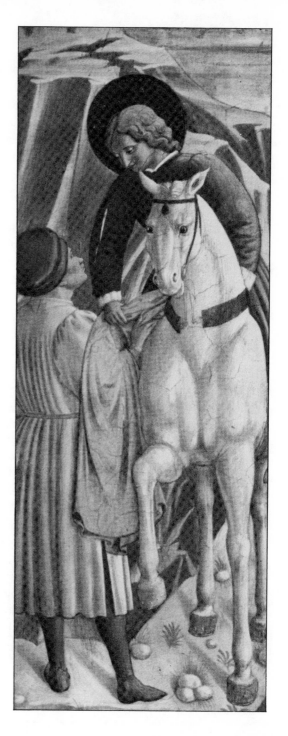

And he gave his coat to a poor man.

fallen in love. This conclusion posed a more delicate question, which, of course, they could not refrain from asking.

"Who is it, Francis, oh, who is it?" his companions demanded to know.

Francis had to answer, but how could he tell them that he was in love with one whom he hardly knew and of whom he was more than a little afraid? So he said to his friends: "I do dream of taking a wife, and she whom I shall marry is so noble, so rich, so fair and so wise, that not one of you has seen her like."

Francis had of late developed a habit of slipping away from the city and entering one of the many caves near Assisi. A friend who saw that Francis was involved in something even more profound than preparations for a wedding, and who had the rare sympathy to keep quiet about it, often accompanied Francis to the retreat. But Francis always entered and stayed alone.

One day he went in and the final surrender was made. He accepted holy poverty as his bride, and on the terms the heavenly Father demanded: the living of the holy gospel.

He emerged from the cave with face flushed and beaming with young love. In his simplicity and youth he perhaps hardly understood what he promised. But sincerely he vowed to fulfill whatever this spouse would demand.

Francis then made a pilgrimage to Rome, emptied his purse in alms-giving, gave his expensive clothes to an eager mendicant, and, dressed in rags, joined a clutch of beggars. He was happy now. He was one with the poor.

After a short time in Rome he returned to Assisi to face a curious temptation. To understand this trial we must remember that the son of Peter Bernardone was a fortunate child of his times. He was brought up to live in a certain social set, to be proud of his manners, neat and fastidious in his clothing and the care of his body. Like all young men he was more sensitive about his physical prowess and appearance than he dared admit.

One by one these principles of his upbringing were to be attacked by the poverty he pledged. He yielded as gracefully as possible to giving away his clothing, joining beggars, and swallowing his fierce Italian pride so that he could beg. But each retreat, each conquest of self, cost him a terrible effort. One thing yet remained for him to surrender and, as he wrote later: "It seemed to me a bitter thing." He must once and for all renounce that body, and his renunciation took a fearful twist.

Europe was, in those days, full of lepers. Feared and despised, these outcasts crept from the edge of one town to another, seeking food and shelter, a bell tied about their necks to warn people of their approach.

One day at a crossroads near Assisi, Francis suddenly came face to face with one of these tragic invalids. Young Francis recoiled in fear and panic, and almost immediately the situation became clear to him. It was, he knew, now or never. He returned to the leper, embraced the astonished outcast, and pressed some money into his broken hands. Francis had now set his course and, typically, he rushed to its logical conclusion. He left that leper and went searching for more lepers and found a hospital full of them. He gathered the amazed pariahs together and begged their pardon for having held them in disgust. He promised to come to them and serve their needs. Giving them what money he had, he kissed each one on the mouth and left.

He was a brave man, this Francis of Assisi.

*   *   *   *   *

If it was money he hated, it was money that did Francis a final service. It broke his connection with his home. One day Francis was passing the tiny, half-ruined chapel of St. Damian just outside Assisi. He entered the place and knelt before a simple Byzantine crucifix to pray. Suddenly the Christus spoke to him and said: "Francis, go and repair My Church, which, as you see, is falling into ruin."

In his utter simplicity Francis accepted the command for what it was. The chapel was in poor condition; it was God's house. Therefore, he reasoned, this is the place I must repair.

His first need was money, and as usual he went to his father. But the merchant had left on a business trip. With some disregard for the Seventh Commandment, Francis went down to the shop, loaded his horse with cloth, and left on his own business trip. He sold the materials and returned to the chapel of St. Damian. The poor aged priest who tended the chapel was set spinning by this impulsive youth. First, the young man kissed his hands, and pressed a sack of gold into them, then announced that he was going to repair the priest's church. Poverty had not dulled the prudence of this priest. He absolutely refused the money and looked with suspicious eye on Francis, whose reputation heretofore had hardly been that of one who worked around the churches.

Nevertheless, the priest permitted Francis to remain and work, but not to use the money.

Francis exercised a bit of prudence of his own. He located a hiding place in the nearby hills against the wrath of his father that was not long in coming.

When Peter Bernardone returned and discovered the theft and flight of his son, he flew from the shop in blind rage and charged toward St. Damian's. Neighbors who had spent days in delicious anticipation of a scene poured into the streets, gesticulating, taking sides, wagging heads, shouting, laughing, sneering—all thoroughly enjoying themselves.

So noisily did this troop bear down on the chapel that Francis heard it in plenty of time to scurry to his hiding place. The priest, whose prudence shines forth as the only sane factor in this insane affair, had made it his business not to know Francis' hideout. He weathered the father's and the crowd's abuse and continued mixing mortar. Long ago he had learned that

San Damiano at Assisi was the first church that Francis restored.

there are situations in which it is best to know, and to say, nothing.

Peter Bernardone—anger now compounded by frustration—stomped back to Assisi with his disappointed audience.

Francis held out for some days and then straggled into town to face the showdown. Assisi must have been shocked when it saw him. Thin and pale, his clothes rough and his hands hard from labor, he looked like a madman. Street urchins began pelting him with rocks and mud, the inevitable crowd gathered (in it were many of his friends) and began jeering and shouting at him. Francis' father heard the uproar, saw who was the center of it, and, completely distraught by the indignities heaped by his son on the good name of the family, tore into the middle of the pack. With shouts, blows and kicks he drove Francis into the house and, to prevent any further nonsense, chained the young man in the cellar.

Some days later the harassed merchant left on another business trip. Francis' long-suffering mother, like so many mothers who seem to love their sons the more for the embarrassments they cause, unchained Francis and let him escape the prison. Like a homing pigeon he flew—right back to St. Damian's.

With this latest insult to his paternal authority, Peter Bernardone's patience gave way. He appealed for civil prosecution of his son. Francis rejected the subsequent summons on the grounds that as a servant of God he was under the jurisdiction of the Bishop of Assisi, Lord Guido. The young man's plea was upheld and the case transferred to ecclesiastical jurisdiction. The Bishop ordered a public trial to be conducted on the plaza in front of the episcopal palace. The family's dirty linen was to be washed in public, and Assisi loved it.

In the episcopal palace, moments before the trial was to take place, Lord Guido explained to Francis the youth's position before the law. "Stealing," the Bishop counseled, "regardless of its purpose, is wrong." He suggested that Francis return what money he had of his father's.

Francis agreed and added: "I will do even more." Stripping himself down to a haircloth about the loins, the intractable young man picked up the heap of clothing and walked onto the plaza to face his father and the curious crowd. If it was a scene the father wanted, Francis' genius was equal to it.

The supreme difference was that the actor was not acting. He was dreadfully and devastatingly sincere.

He cried out: "Listen well, all of you—until now I called Peter Bernardone 'father.' But now that I wish to serve God I return to him not only his money that he so much desires, but the clothes, too, that I had from him." Francis threw the clothing and the money in a heap on the plaza. "Now I will truly be able to say 'Our Father who art in heaven,' and not 'My father Peter Bernardone.' "

Now a more shameful thing happened. Peter Bernardone bent down and scooped up the money and the clothing and left, hurling curses and anathemas over his shoulder. The trial was over.

Clad only in a threadbare gardener's cloak which the Bishop had given him to cover himself, Francis left Assisi. He headed into the mountains surrounding the town—just why, it is difficult to say. Many times in his life he experienced an almost overwhelming hunger for solitude. No doubt after the bitter events on Assisi's plaza he needed time to sort things out.

His sojourn in the mountains, however, was far from tranquil. A band of thieves ambushed him and, finding he had nothing, threw him into a ravine full of snow. Wet and cold, Francis climbed up out of the snowy cleft and made his way to a monastery, where the monks gave him shelter—and precious little else—in exchange for his labors as a kitchen boy. Sheer cold and hunger drove Francis from this inhospitable monastery. He journeyed to Gubbio, a village near Assisi, where an old friend of his gave the suffering, but quietly cheerful young man a cast-off hermit's habit. Thus clad, Francis returned to St. Damian's and continued the restoration of the ruin.

Money he had none, but rocks, mortar, wood, and other basic materials he begged in Assisi, along with what food he and the priest needed. Gradually the barrage of jibes and curses and pelting died out as the townsfolk got used to Francis.

One must not judge these Assisians too harshly. Francis had, after all, not only stolen, defied paternal love and authority (however wrongly that authority had been used), but also was continuing his contacts with the lepers. That these people dealt with him at all is a tribute to them.

At any rate, it appears that from this compost of family fights, public

Among the relics of St. Francis, preserved in the
Basilica of St. Francis, are his shoes.

scenes and threats of contagion, the flowers of natural Italian courtesy finally
asserted themselves.

Francis was the main reason for the change of attitude. With piercing
knowledge of his own sins, he refused to consider the insults and rocks hurled
at him as anything other than what he deserved. Those who perpetrated

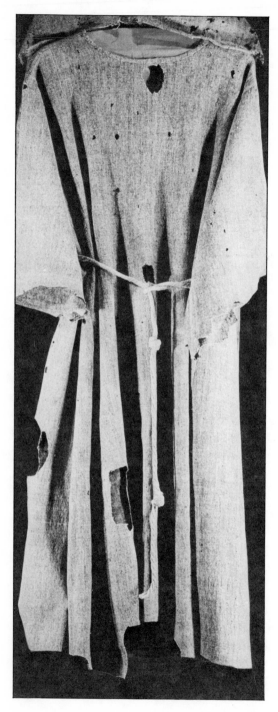

According to tradition,
this is the tunic Francis wore when
he was at the point of death.

these actions he saw as friends who had the courage to tell him the truth. If he had braved these storms with a grim, stiff-upper-lip attitude, he would no doubt have further enraged his neighbors. As a result of the honest conviction of his own sinfulness, however, he bore his ostracism joyfully and courteously.

And while he had chosen a bitter road for himself, he despised no one for not following him, nor did he urge anyone to join him. In short, he minded his own mysterious business.

And so it became a pleasant thing to see Francis. A meeting with him somehow made one's whole day brighter. And the sweet blessing he offered when one gave him a stone, a bit of bread, a piece of wood, rose from his heart. "Give me a stone," he would cry, "and God will bless you. Give me two stones and God will twice bless you."

For Francis, the relief of having finally left his broken road of compromise for the broad highways of poverty was so great that he could not help but enjoy himself. In a ferment of love for his lady poverty he would often bubble out into song. From sheer exuberance he formed a mock violin from two pieces of wood and sang the praises of his wonderful God and God's daughter lady poverty.

For the next two or three years Francis restored chapels (he did at least three), begged food and materials and served the lepers.

And then, God complicated his life.

While Francis was hearing Mass on the feast of St. Matthias, 1209, in St. Mary of the Angels—one of his restored chapels—almighty God revealed, through the Gospel read on that feast (Matthew 10: 7-19), the full life's work of the cloth merchant's son. After Mass Francis asked the priest to explain this Gospel to him. The priest told him it meant that the disciples of Christ must possess nothing—neither money, food, nor excess clothing. They were simply to preach the kingdom of God and penance for sin.

These words of the inspired Matthew were the catalyst that brought the Franciscan movement into being.

Francis trembled with enthusiasm and exclaimed: "This is what I long with all my inmost heart to do." In his devastating directness, he cast off what he considered excess clothing—his shoes, belt, mantle. He wore now a simple tunic bound about his middle with a cord. Later the chill of the Italian winter forced him (he was never of robust health) to wear a cloak, but it was one he made himself.

He began to preach before the people of Assisi—an act of supreme humility. Knowing that his people were busy, he made his sermons brief and simple.

His natural charm and warm, sympathetic personality became a vehicle of God's grace. His goodness lay naked before Assisi, and to its everlasting credit Assisi accepted him for what he was.

Within the next year, 11 men slipped silently from various strata of society and asked to be his companions, and to live as he lived. Some brought talents, others money, others nothing much but their sins. He took them all on condition that they give away everything: their money to the poor, their wills to a superior (they took turns as superior), and that they struggle to overcome their sins.

These first followers were the first children of his own marriage to lady poverty. There would be more and more until the end of time. One night in a dream he saw them,

> . . . a great multitude of men . . . ; their footfalls
> still resound in my ears as they come and go according to the
> commands of holy obedience. The highroads are crowded
> with them, coming to this place (Assisi), from almost every
> nation. There are Frenchmen coming, Spaniards hurrying,
> Germans and Englishmen running, and a tremendous throng
> speaking various other tongues hastens here.

In 1209 Francis wrote a Rule of Life for his present and future brethren. Composed of Gospel texts and some very few precepts, this Rule aimed at guiding these men to walk literally in the footsteps of Christ.

This concept of the literal imitation of Christ demanded a departure from forms of religious life known in the Catholic Church up to the time of Francis. For many centuries the monastic system had effectively served (and still does serve) the church. Monasteries were well-established institutions within whose cloisters and lands men (monks) sought religious perfection, by living a well-ordered routine of work and prayer. While each monk took his vows of obedience, chastity and poverty, the monastery as a legal entity was able to own things. The monks supported themselves by the fruits of their own industry. Always advancing as disciplined, orderly, organized colonies of Christ, the monks preserved and propagated the Catholic religion in Europe throughout the horrors of barbarian invasion and the feudal wars.

Francis, however, saw the world as his followers' monastery. Rather than bind them to the exquisitely organized cloisters of monastic discipline, he was inspired by God, and the needs of his times, to send them into the frightfully disorganized world. If the world was their cloister, their bodies were their cells. Food and clothing were not to be their problem, for the heavenly Father who sent them was to provide for their needs. They were to live the gospel and by their own poverty and humility give Christlike example to men suffering under the burden of sin. Their work was to be whatever the needs of the church demanded. Francis called his followers the Little Brothers, *Frati Minori,* a name which has come down to us today in the title Friars Minor.

Catholic that he was, Francis insisted on seeking the approval of this form of life from Pope Innocent III. In 1209 he set out with his by now 12 followers for Rome.

Innocent was understandably reluctant when Francis first presented his case. Rome is, after all, the seat of prudence, and when a comparatively unknown youth enters the papal chambers seeking universal approval of a novel form of religious life, the prudent thing would seem to be to ignore him and it. And it appears that Innocent acted prudently.

But even popes sleep and even popes dream, and during the night after his interview with Francis, Innocent dreamt a strange dream. He saw the huge Roman basilica of St. John Lateran, the Mother Church of Christendom, quaking on its ancient foundations, threatening to lean over and fall as a great tree before a storm. Suddenly a little man appeared and threw his thin body against the toppling structure and alone held it up before the nameless furies threatening it. The face of the little man was plain: it was that of Innocent's petitioner of the day before.

It would not be prudent for a pope to change a decision on the basis of a dream, but he sent for Francis, and listened to him far more carefully. Like every other human being, Innocent was touched by the personality before him. But because prudence subordinates personalities to principles, Innocent consulted his advisers. They concluded with the Pope that Francis' revolutionary ideas had merit and further to deny their validity would be to deny

"Suddenly a little man appeared and threw his thin body against the toppling structure and alone held it up."

Clare joins Francis, and the Poor Clares become the contemplative
branch of the Franciscan Order.

that one could live a life described as ideal in the gospels. Innocent gave his verbal endorsement and promised more definite approval if Francis' plan proved practical.

Ten years later Francis' order numbered more than 3,000 men.

Returning to Assisi with papal approval for their way of life, the friars took up quarters in an abandoned mule shed until a thoughtless peasant, wishing to shelter his mule, drove the friars out. Francis led them back to St. Mary of the Angels (called the Portiuncula, i. e., the Little Portion); and this little chapel, given to the friars by Benedictine monks, became their headquarters. They lived in tiny mud huts around it, continued their prayers and mortifications, their preaching and labors, and other men continued to come and join them.

It was during this period of his life that Francis established his Second Order of contemplative women, known as the Poor Clares, and perhaps, too, his Third Order for men and women living in the world.

Francis had no trouble with men who wished to follow his type of life, but what could he do with a woman? And a woman whose blood was noble and whose will was steel. Her name was Clare di Favorone and she was 18 years of age.

Clare had probably heard Francis preach on various occasions in Assisi, and one day she confided her difficulties to him. She explained her reasons for not marrying. She not only desired to give her life and love completely to God, but also had determined to live in the same poverty as Francis and his brethren. Within a short time Clare made her decision to break with the world and her family—and to follow the road Francis mapped out for her.

On Palm Sunday evening of the year 1212, while the family was dining, Clare slipped out a back door (tradition says it was the "Door of the Dead"—the exit reserved in Umbrian households for the sole purpose of carrying out the family dead), and in the darkness of the night met another kinswoman and accomplice, the Lady Pacifica. The two women then made their way to the chapel of St. Mary of the Angels, where Francis and some of the other friars awaited them. By candlelight, Francis snipped off Clare's long golden tresses. Pacifica slipped a rough brown robe over Clare's feast day dress, fastened it around her waist with a rope, and then covered her

This silver case holds the blonde curls of St. Clare. The relic is
preserved in the Basilica of St. Clare.

shorn head with a black veil. Clare pronounced her vows of poverty, chastity
and obedience to almighty God. In this romantic and improbable fashion
the Second Order of St. Francis, known as the Poor Clares—or the Poor
Ladies of Assisi—made its entrance into the history of the world.

As the years passed, the fame of Francis and his friars spread throughout Italy. The leaven was at work in the masses. His arrival in the little towns
was always an occasion of great celebration. Bells would ring, people would
shout, run and tumble on waves of joyous enthusiasm to the plaza to hear and
see him. This was no reformer who moved in a cloud of gloom. He bubbled
with life, and the Italians, as sensitive to mood and personality as leaves to
a breeze, rejoiced with him. He never argued with heretics, flailed at sinners,
or pleaded for divine vengeance. Rather, he spoke to them courteously and
simply of virtues and vices and of the Christ he saw in each of them. His

penetrating sense of the presence of God touched not only human hearts, but swept on to produce incredible responses on every level of animate and inanimate nature.

All creation was for Francis a proof of the goodness of God, and the universe was Christ's kingdom. It seemed as if God had restored to this little poor man the mastery over nature that Adam had surrendered in paradise.

*   *   *   *   *

Francis knew few fears in his life, but there was one that constantly plagued him. And that was fear of becoming a hypocrite. He knew that the best sermons his friars could preach would be the example of their own lives, and he was painfully aware that the validity of his mission to restore the gospel as a way of life for all would rest on his ability to live it himself. Once when he was ill (as he often was) his superior ordered him to sew a piece of fox fur inside his habit against the cold. He obeyed but pleaded for and was granted permission to sew another piece on the outside of the habit so that people could see how Francis of Assisi pampered himself.

To understand Francis' success as a religious reformer one must grasp the utter simplicity of his movement. Religious reform, he insisted, must begin with one's self, and he demanded this of every man who joined his order. While indeed gentle with human weaknesses, Francis bided no deviation from the ideal on the part of the friars. His way of life, he felt, was simple enough—to live the gospel. With any other schemes, plans, tables of organization, he had, at this point in his life, little patience.

It is significant that while Francis passionately loved all of nature, he could never quite warm up to ants. They were simply too tightly organized and frantically industrious to suit him. His order as he conceived it could hardly be dignified with the term "organization." It simply existed to give the world an example of Christlike living. The specifics he preferred to leave to circumstances of time and place and the considerable ingenuity of his friars. Love, he knew, must always find a way to manifest itself.

We are told that St. Dominic, who brilliantly organized the then new Order of Preachers (Dominicans), attempted to persuade Francis to unite

the Friars Minor with his Friar Preachers and form one great order. What the Franciscans patently lacked—namely, refined and efficient organization—Dominic Guzman knew he could provide. Dominic must have thrilled at the possibilities of such a union, but Francis, who could charm, was never easily charmed. He was too simple, and too certain of the role Christ wished his order to assume in the church. He rejected the great Dominic's proposal. But it is the measure of the humble Spaniard that the rejection of his plan destroyed neither his respect nor affection for Francis. The two founders, according to tradition, were close friends. The friendship, unique in the church, has continued between their orders for more than 700 years.

By 1217, however, the order had grown to such proportions that Francis had to impose some vague outlines of organization. He established territorial divisions (provinces) and superiors. But the saint insisted that the chain of command he forged be not of the steel of obedience, but of the fire of love. Hence he called his superiors neither prior, abbot or superior, but ministers and defined their duties as servants of the rest of the brethren.

Dominic (right) and Francis met at the 4th Lateran Council in 1215 and talked of merging their Orders.

Each Pentecost and also at Michaelmas (near the end of September) Francis called the friars back to Assisi for a general gathering or chapter. At these reunions the policies of the order, its development, its various other problems, were discussed.

It was at the Pentecost Chapter of 1217 that Francis decided to send brethren outside Italy—to both pagan and Christian lands. Humanly speaking, his organizing was the usual shambles. In these days, when missioners study everything from architecture to zoology, it is shocking to realize that one of the greatest, most sustained missionary efforts in the Catholic Church began with men who simply volunteered and went. Superiors were chosen and friars moved out on foot to France, Spain, Germany, Hungary, Portugal, Syria and the Near East. Within 100 years from the date of this chapter, more than 30,000 Friars Minor were living in all parts of Europe. And Franciscans had penetrated and successfully established missions in the uncharted and pagan kingdoms of the Near, Middle and Far East.

Two years after the Chapter of 1217, Francis himself left Italy on one of the most incredible missionary ventures in the annals of the church. He journeyed to Damietta, Egypt, where the crusaders were locked in vicious no-quarter warfare with the Saracens. There he crossed the battle lines, somehow survived inside the Saracen camp, and procured an interview with Melek-el-kamel, Sultan and commander in chief of the Mussulman forces. He proposed that the Sultan be baptized a Christian. Surprisingly enough, the Sultan gave serious consideration to Francis' plea. Finally, he reluctantly rejected the proposal, knowing that his countrymen would take a dim view of such a defection. Nevertheless he did grant Francis and his followers permission to journey and preach throughout Egypt. It was at this time that Francis visited the Holy Land and prayed at those places made sacred by the presence of Christ.

*   *   *   *   *

Five friars left Portiuncula to go to Morocco, passing through Alamquer, present-day Seville. Proclaiming themselves to be the ambassadors of the King of Kings, Jesus Christ, they were put into chains and dispatched to

Morocco. Here, naked, "they intrepidly confessed and proclaimed their faith." They were cruelly yoked by their necks and dragged along the ground like sacks. The king promised to save their lives and provide them with money and women if they would convert to Islam. In reply, they proclaimed their contempt for all earthly things. So, grabbing a sword, the king himself beheaded them on the spot. When told of this, Francis exclaimed: "God be praised! Now I truly know I have five minor brothers!"

Meanwhile the order continued its uninhibited growth. But with the rapid expansion came a series of crosses and complications that threatened to destroy the work Francis had so effectively begun.

The pioneer days, when a small number of friars drew their inspiration from regular contact with their founder, had ended. Now, with the order numbering thousands and already sinking its roots in foreign soil, many a friar had never even met Francis, much less had the opportunity to draw inspiration from contact with him. It became increasingly evident that more detailed legislation must be provided if the Order of Little Brothers was to fulfill its mission in the church.

Summoned back from the Holy Land to face these problems of growth, Francis called a General Chapter for the year 1220. At the chapter he resigned as Minister General, so that he could devote himself entirely to preparing a more detailed rule of life for his friars.

The next three years, during which Francis labored to develop the Franciscan Rule, were a period of great stress in his life. Although not well equipped by temperament or training to be a lawmaker, he had set himself a formidable legislative goal. He determined to produce a rule that would permit his friars to live the holy gospel with the greatest amount of individual liberty and the minimum of regulation.

Francis' burden was not lightened by certain vocal elements among the friars who entertained their own ideas regarding future development of the order and Francis' ability to guide it. It seems poetically just that during these days and years of trial, the Holy See, which Francis and his friars had already done so much to foster and strengthen, bent down to help lift up its little servants from their own confusion. Cardinal Hugolino (later Pope Gregory IX) became, at Francis' request, protector of the order and guided

Francis to the completion of the Rule of 1223, which the order observes to this day.

The struggle to prevent the dissolution of his order, to salvage his ideals, and keep them at the core and center of his new Franciscan Rule of Life (which he did)—all this exacted its inexorable toll on the already fragile health of Francis.

He began to realize that he was coming near the end of his course on earth.

As the Angel of Death (he called it Sister Death) hovered ever closer to him, he became obsessed with one idea. He had lived more like Christ than any man before or since; now he begged to die like Christ. And he knew that this would demand a miracle.

In August, 1224, he retired with some few friars to a mountain called Alvernia in Umbria, near Assisi, to spend time in prayer. The Italian summer days softened one into another as the saint entered into a mystical union with Christ that we dare not even attempt to describe. So intense were the exchanges of love that Francis begged to share with Christ the sufferings of Calvary. Frightful as the re-

The view along the valley of Tescio toward Assisi. The rock fortress marks the heights where Francis was born.

quest was, Christ granted it, and in an awesome vision, the Crucified Christ embraced him and poured into Francis' soul—and his fragile body—the black horrors of the first Good Friday. When Francis stepped back from this embrace he saw his miracle. Christ had cut into his body the same five wounds he had suffered on the cross. They were the red seals of divine approval pressed into the hands and feet and side of Francis of Assisi.

During the last two years of his life the little poor man's cup of physical suffering was filled up, pressed down, and ran over. His health broke. Spleen, liver, stomach and eyes throbbed in the discordant rhythm of pain. His whole system was lashed by recurrent bouts of the malaria he had contracted in Egypt. Efforts of physicians to comfort and cure him, if sincere, were most crude. The doctors, for instance, applied red-hot irons to his temples to relieve the pain in his eyes—an ordeal he endured with grace because Brother Fire had acknowledged Francis' plea not to hurt him.

But it was during these last days, when nature had marshaled most vicious forces to destroy him, that Francis looked into the shimmering curtains of pain and saw his bodily antagonist for what it really was—the gift of God to man. As his spirit rose above the crags and peaks of pain, he pulled what rags of bodily strength were left about him and broke into his own song to nature, the magnificent Canticle of the Sun.

There was not merely something of the poet, knight and saint in Francis, there was everything of him in him. Poet, knight and saint he was to the last—this simple, courageous man.

It was during his illness that Francis felt a greater need to sing than ever before. Nothing assuaged his pain like the sound of a stanza of verse. Therefore he continually asked his attendant friars to intone lauds and psalms. He wanted to die in a state of gladness because gladness is the fruit of sanctity.

Friar Elias chided him gently: he was concerned about public opinion. "How can you show so much gaiety when you should be thinking of death?" he asked Francis. Francis replied: "I have been thinking of my end night and day for so long! From the time you had that vision in Foligno and you told me that I had only two more years to live, from that time I have never ceased to think about death. Let me now rejoice in the Lord and in the praises sung to Him for my infirmities. . ."

The end came October 3, 1226, towards sundown. He died singing.

Francis receives the stigmata—the impression of the five
wounds of Christ on his body.

7. St. John Bosco

Turin, a gracious Northern Italian city nestled at the feet of the Alps' snowcapped peaks, had seen better days than those of the winter of 1846. So skillfully had ancient Roman engineers designed the town's main streets and squares that for centuries travelers praised Turin as "the loveliest village in the world." Many aristocratic families traced their ancestry to the days when Roman legions, garrisoned at Turin, had guarded Italy's northern reaches and controlled the Alpine passes through which commerce, and occasionally invading armies, moved into Italy.

With this magnificent scenic setting, cultured population, and commercial importance, the city, very early in its history, developed a distinct aristocratic style. In the mid-19th century the House of Savoy, royal rulers of Northern Italy, held court there.

But all was not serene. Like so many European and American cities, Turin was changing from a quiet provincial center into a busy industrial town. As more and more factories sprang up, more and more people flowed from Northern Italy's farms and out of the Alpine valleys to seek employment and excitement. Turin's new aristocrats, the industrial overlords, uninhibited

John's birthplace at Becchi. His mother left this peaceful farm to join
her son, and sold her wedding gown to support his work.

by any social legislation, overworked and underpaid their ignorant and un-
sophisticated workers. The city of broad boulevards, charming squares, and
covered arcades now developed a new feature, slums. The recently arrived
working class crowded into filthy, airless tenements, sometimes six or eight
to a room. Vice, disease, and crime flourished; for most slum dwellers God
was a dim memory associated with the farms or dairies they had abandoned
for the city. Vicious gangs of young toughs formed in the streets and often
invaded Turin's better sections, leaving a trail of robberies, muggings, and
occasionally murder in their wake.

"Law and order!" cried Turin's citizens.

City fathers increased the police force, and administered justice swiftly, if not always fairly. The "loveliest village in the world," now claiming a
population of 150,000 people, boasted no fewer than four good-sized prisons.

Many inmates were mere boys, some not yet in their teens.

Another problem plagued Turin's harassed citizenry. At its root was, of all things, a slightly offbeat priest. For the past several years this strange cleric, known as Don (Father) John Bosco, had been leading a band of singing, shouting, scabrous slum boys through Turin's stylish streets, usually to Sunday outings in the country. The priest, clad in battered biretta, patched cassock, and peasant workshoes, had first started with a handful of boys. Now the original pack had swollen into a horde numbering some four hundred. Although the boys had not yet committed any crime, citizens worried about Bosco's ability to control his small army.

Fellow clergymen judged that Don Bosco was acting out some Napoleonic fantasy. Two of them attempted to commit him to Turin's insane asylum. The move backfired when Bosco cleverly maneuvered asylum guards into taking his two clerical adversaries instead of himself.

Government authorities, newspaper editors, and enemies of the church feared that Father Bosco was laying the foundations of a future political power base. In Italy's then sulphurous political climate such an assumption was not unreasonable. The Italy of Father Bosco's time was not the united country we know today. It was divided into seven different states. Austrian and French royal houses ruled a good half of the nation.

The papal states, ruled by Pope Pius IX, straddled the nation's central portion. When Pius IX, who had no army, refused to support a war to throw out the Austrian occupiers, many Italians judged the Pontiff a defender of foreign rulers and an opponent of national unity. The vast tide of anticlericalism which had been building for years swept over the land. Enemies of the Church drove bishops from their dioceses, suppressed religious houses and exiled priests, sisters and brothers.

Pope Pius IX and the Italian clergy became the favorite whipping boys of the liberal revolutionary press. Hatred reached a boiling point when revolutionary gangs in November, 1848, broke into Pope Pius IX's Roman palace, stabbed his prime minister, and fatally shot one of the Pope's staff. Slipping out a secret door, Pope Pius IX fled to the kingdom of Naples, where he remained in exile for six months.

Because of the nature of his work and the success he had already enjoyed with youth, Don Bosco became a favorite target of anticlericals. To all charges he calmly replied: "I side with the Pope in matters of religion. In politics I side with no one. . . . I am a priest. The only kingdom I serve is the Kingdom of God."

John had been yearning to serve that kingdom since he was a small boy. "At the age of nine," he wrote, "I knew I wanted to be a priest and to help boys." He had no easy time in making his dream come true. His father, a hardworking farmer, died when John was not yet two years old. His mother, Margaret, held her family together, running the small Bosco farm, raising three children, and supporting her own elderly and infirm mother. Margaret, a woman of sterling character and enormous courage, proved equal to the relentless and often bitter struggle to survive.

Despite their poverty, Margaret encouraged John to build his dream—to serve the kingdom of God.

Although lacking money and influence, young John Bosco was not without resources. He possessed an amazing array of talents. His physical coordination, even as a youngster, was superb. At country fairs he studied the magician's tricks and the daredevil's acrobatic stunts. Back home he practiced these feats until he could imitate and often excel his mentors. Although suffering many a bruise and sprain in the process, John never lost his enthusiasm for his dangerous recreation. He knew magic tricks and tightrope balancing would attract young people to him.

Margaret Bosco.

His physical prowess, however, pales before his mental acumen. Highly intelligent, John possessed a memory that combined the best features of a tape recorder and a copying machine. This talent came to light one evening when, during the course of a parish mission, the pastor inquired if John understood the missionary's sermon. The little boy of only nine years repeated without mistake every word the missionary had preached. And this was in the day when no missionary would dare descend from the pulpit unless he poured it on for at least an hour!

As John grew to young manhood he reached medium height. His face, open and frank, was crowned by a rich crop of curly chestnut hair. He was cheerful, disciplined, and had a tremendous capacity for work.

Young Bosco had his faults, too. Even as a young man, his feelings and emotions ran deep and strong. He could be impetuous; he was not above, on a rare occasion, settling problems with his fists. He judged himself so full of self-pride that he deeply feared he would use his future position as a parish priest to feed his cravings for prestige. So successfully, however, did John keep all these forces within him under control that calmness and peacefulness characterized his whole life and his relationships with others.

John had to work very hard for his seminary education. During the long years of study he picked up a variety of jobs and learned, incidentally, a host of trades. Before reaching ordination he could make candy, repair shoes, design and mend suits, manage a restaurant, and put on a one-man circus. The latter he loved. His showmanship attracted the small fry. After he had the little ones suitably awed, he'd slip in a catechism lesson or two.

In 1841 Turin's Archbishop Fransoni ordained John, now 25, for his archdiocese. Shortly after ordination the Archbishop approved Bosco for an intensive five-year course of postgraduate theology at Turin's Ecclesiastical College.

College authorities, aware that many Italian priests refused to mix with the people because of the anticlerical hatred, insisted that the young theology scholars mix with the city's population, particularly its poor elements. Thus John visited and worked in the hospitals, prisons, orphanages, and slum sections. This firsthand experience with cultured Turin's grubby underside shocked his sensitive and gentle heart.

John renovated the Pinardi house to accommodate the large number of
boys he taught and sheltered.

It was, however, the young slum boys' plight that bothered him most.
At nine years of age, John had dreamed of becoming a priest. He had accomplished this. Now he had to make real the second part of the dream—to serve boys.

He started. When still a theological student, he persuaded a few youngsters to meet with him Sunday afternoons at the College courtyard. Patiently he established a relationship with the street kids based on the famous saying of St. Francis de Sales: "You can catch more flies with honey than with vinegar."

Catch flies he did. Apprentice brought apprentice; street arab brought street arab, orphan brought orphan. As John moved through Turin's slums he invited youngsters to his Sunday get-togethers at the College. He called these gatherings his "oratory." The oratory featured singing, prayer, and catechism as well as horseplay, contests, long walks, and picnics. A pioneer disciple remembered those pleasant Sundays.

> At the end of each Sunday excursion, Father Bosco always told us to plan for next Sunday. The roads, the programs, and the hour. He gave us advice as to our conduct and asked us—if we had any friends—to invite them, too. . . . Joy reigned among us. Those happy days are engraved in our memories and influenced our future lives. Arriving at some church in the precincts of town, Don Bosco would ask permission of the parish priest to celebrate Mass. The permission was always granted, and then at a signal the noisy band gathered together to attend in a spirit of oneness which amazed the bystanders. Catechism followed breakfast: the grass and rocks supplied the plates and tables. It is true, bread failed now and then, but gaiety never. . . . We recited the rosary while walking, and at sunset we marched back again into Turin. We were fatigued, but our hearts were content.

Not everyone in Turin was content. Indeed, John, having completed his College residency, could find no place to gather his boys who now numbered 400. Some generous people did try to help. But the noise and sheer presence of this huge, energetic band overwhelmed them and often brought neighbors' wrath down on their heads. No fewer than 10 people within a space of five months had offered John the use of their facilities. Every one of them, after a few experiences with the oratory, withdrew his promise. Father Bosco simply had no place to gather his ragged flock. Later, remembering Palm Sunday of 1846, when John felt his work might come to an end, he wrote:

> As I looked at the crowd of children and the thought of the rich harvest they promised my priesthood, I felt my heart was breaking. I was alone, without helpers. My health was shattered, and I could not tell where to gather my poor little lambs any more.

John urged his little ones to pray; and as so often happened, his youngsters' prayers were answered. A certain Mr. Pinardi offered to rent John a piece of property located in Turin's marshy area, called the *Valdocco*—"Valley of the Ducks." John, still stinging from his recent defeats, was slow to respond. Pinardi pointed out that his property contained a small hayshed which John could use for a chapel. When John saw the shed he was bitterly disappointed. It was simply too low for him to enter. "Oh, good Father, do not worry," counseled the irrepressible Pinardi. "We will dig down and lower the shed's floor. You will have Mass here on Easter Sunday."

Pinardi was as good as his word. On Easter Sunday morning John celebrated Mass at a humble altar surrounded by his urchins, who had jammed into the rickety shack. Pinardi's shed was no Sistine Chapel and the young workers no Sistine choir. But that did not stop them from celebrating their Easter Mass with gusto. John was happy. The oratory finally had a home. The priest did not yet know he was to pay a fearful price for his success.

*   *   *   *   *

For five years, even during his theology studies, John had dedicated his life to his youngsters. Although he met with them as a group only on Sundays, every spare moment he had during the week he gave to meeting their needs. He visited them at their jobs, found work for those laid off, nursed the sick, assisted those who had run afoul of the law. Using every possible means, John struggled to keep his little ones out of Turin's corrupting reformatories.

But all this caught up with him when, three months after purchasing the Pinardi place, John, near exhaustion, suffered a severe pneumonia attack. At the hospital where he was taken, doctors feared for his life. Heartbroken and bewildered boys, on hearing the news, milled about the hospital courtyard, hoping for further information. Many youngsters straggled into a nearby church and lifting tearstained faces to heaven, prayed for this man who loved them so much. Leadership sprang up from their ranks, and holy hours and all-night vigils were organized.

In their youthful enthusiasm the boys hurled stern promises heavenward. More than one vowed to reform his life, say extra prayers, and do penance. Some little construction workers, whose job demanded they carry bricks and mortar up four or five stories of scaffolding 40 or 50 times a day, fasted from solid foods. Although these children suffered pain and came near fainting, they were determined to wrestle John Bosco out of death's grip by their prayers and penances.

All their efforts, however, seemed doomed to failure. As his condition continued to worsen, John prepared to die, and received the last rites. At his bedside, Father Borel, a close friend, bent over John and whispered: "John, these children need you. Ask God to let you stay. Please, say this prayer after me, 'Lord, if it be your good pleasure, cure me. I say this prayer in the name of my children.'" John repeated the prayer. When he finished it his fever broke. The pneumonia crisis had passed.

Two weeks later doctors released John from the hospital. In the courtyard outside, his black sheep awaited him. When Don Bosco appeared, they rushed him, picked him up, and carried him on their shoulders through Turin's streets. Filled with joy, they sang, shouted, and cheered. Even the city's proper citizens were moved to tears. These street arabs and gutter children proved their magnificent loyalty and devotion to their Father.

John sat patiently for hours in his office listening to those who came for his wise counsel.

Until a short time before his illness, a wealthy noblewoman, the Marchioness of Barolo, had provided John's living quarters in Turin. When the priest, absorbed in his own work, refused to direct one of her ladyship's pet charities, a girls' orphanage, she ordered John out of the apartment. So, when he came from the hospital, he actually had no place to lay his head. It was no pressing problem, however, for he had decided to go to his mother's home in the farm country some 20 miles outside Turin, for a period of recuperation.

When John returned to the city, the indefatigable Mr. Pinardi once more appeared and offered to rent John four rooms in an apartment of his bordering the oratory property. Because this particular house and its neighboring dwellings had an unsavory reputation, Bosco hesitated. Finally, reasoning that his mother's presence would lessen suspicion of his own activities, John asked Margaret to make the painful sacrifice of leaving the farm life she loved, to be a housemother in the narrow confines of a city apartment.

"Do you think it is God's will?" she asked her son. "Yes, Mother, I do," responded John. That was all Margaret needed, and in November of 1846 she gathered their poor possessions and set out with her son for the city. The two, mother and son, walked the entire 20 miles from farm to city, because they had no money for transportation.

Soon after John's mother arrived at the oratory, the children dubbed her "Mama Margaret." Bosco would often say to her, "Mother, someday this whole place will be a playground, with schoolrooms, workshops; there will be clerics and a world of children." Mama, aware of John's natural exuberance, listened skeptically to her son. All the priest had was a piece of land of dubious value, a half-underground chapel, an apartment in a building that was contributing significantly to Turin's urban blight, and a weekend invasion of some 600 boys in varying degrees of disrepair. But John was determined to establish a world of children, and he would build that world step by step.

He determined first of all to provide a solid practical education for his boys. Starting at ground zero, he taught the three R's. Since religious instruction was essential to his education program, John selected a simple catechism for his students' reading primer. He first held classes in his Pinardi apartment. As more and more students came, they overflowed the tiny rooms into the chapel and the sacristy. Even this was not enough and John finally persuaded Mr. Pinardi to rent him the whole house.

The curriculum expanded apace. To the original three R's, John soon added geography, grammar, and drawing. He also added singing, stating that "an oratory without singing is like a body without a soul."

To ensure a steady supply of teachers for his ever-expanding school, John worked out an agreement with some of the school's more gifted students. He trained them in secondary studies, Italian, literature, Latin, French, and mathematics, with the understanding that they would, in turn, teach for a period of time in the grammar school. The arrangement benefited both John and his teaching staff. Don Bosco had a fine faculty drawn from the ranks of the pupil-teachers of the oratory itself. The new teachers now had sufficient education to enter studies that would lead to professional careers. Thus they could break the cycle of poverty into which many of them had been born.

Within a year of settling on the Pinardi property, John had between six and seven hundred children under instruction, ranging anywhere from eight to 18 and some few on either side of those ages. These earnest youngsters jammed every available inch of space in the Pinardi house and the chapel. John refused to turn anyone away. Yet there was simply no more room.

Undismayed, John summoned the whole oratory one night and resolved the crisis. "When a beehive overflows," he explained, "it swarms, and its surplus goes out to fill another hive. And so it is with us. In playtime we are all upon one another; at chapel we are packed like herrings in a barrel. There is no room to move. Let us copy the bees and go and seek another oratory." The fact that he had no money did not disturb him at all. He knew God would provide. As usual he was right. Not one, but two oratories soon opened in Turin.

* * * * *

One cold rainy night in May, 1847, Margaret responded to a tap on the Pinardi house door. A little waif, wet to the bone, stood trembling from the chill, on the steps. Margaret immediately brought the child in, set him

before a roaring fire, dried him, fed him, and then put him to bed. He turned
out to be "the boy who came to dinner." He was an orphan, and his gentle
knock opened a whole new door for Don Bosco. The plight of Turin's
orphaned and homeless boys had borne heavily on Don Bosco's heart since
his arrival in the city. Now John felt he could do something about it. It was
not long before the new arrival was joined by ten other little fellows whom
John somehow stuffed into the Pinardi house. After the winter of 1851,
when he finally purchased the Pinardi house, John was able to accept some
30 boarders. The house lived by a wondrous routine. In the morning, after
John had celebrated Mass for the youngsters, they would depart for their
workshop or factory, a little snack in their hands. At noon they would return and crowd into the kitchen for their noonday dinner, which John, the
cook, had prepared and, now clad in a white apron, served them. The little

Bosco hearing the confession of Paul Albera, who
eventually became the third superior of the Salesians. Bosco believed
confession to be an important part of his education program,
the opportunity to guide the spiritual development of the young people.

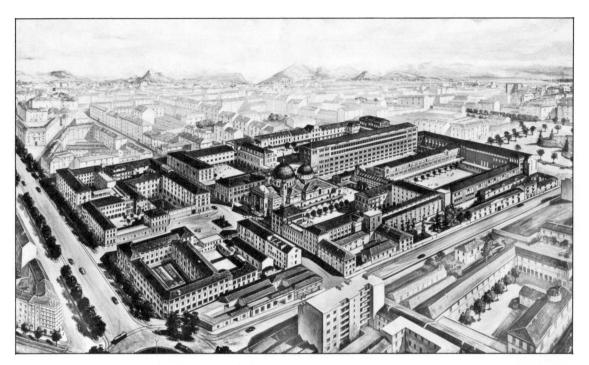

John Bosco's Oratory in Turin started with a small wooden shed.

boys would depart for afternoon work and return in the evening for supper; then Professor Bosco would supervise their lessons.

The increased activity, however, took its toll on Mama Margaret, now in her mid-60's. She toiled all day long, cleaning house, washing and mending clothes, nursing the boys who were ill. Boys being boys, their carelessness often caused poor Margaret much extra work. One day, fed up with her clothesline being knocked down, her vegetable garden trampled, weary from endless washing, mending and cooking, Mama Margaret announced to her son: "I'm going home."

Don Bosco felt his mother's anguish. He said nothing. He simply pointed to a crucifix hanging on the wall. His mother understood and her eyes filled with tears. "You are right, son; you are right," she said softly. Mama Margaret replaced her apron.

*   *   *   *   *

John encouraged the production of concerts and plays at the Oratory, an endeavor contrary to the practices of the stern moralists of the day.

As quickly as John finished one project he began another. In rapid succession he built a boarding home for 150 boys, a new chapel to accommodate the oratory's increased enrollment, and pioneered evening education and vocational schools for his future craftsmen and artisans. He built shoemaker, tailor, carpenter, bookbinder, printing and ironwork shops. Once again he chose his faculty from boys who had come through the oratory. His schools, considered among Turin's best, took their inspiration and direction from Don Bosco himself, who ranks among modern Europe's finest educators. A colleague, a distinguished professor, explains why. "His love shone forth from his looks and his words so clearly, and all felt it and could not doubt it. . . . They experienced an immense joy when in his presence."

John demanded much from his teachers. At a time when schoolmasters considered blows and whipping an indispensable tool of their trade,

Don Bosco forbade any such violence. "Make yourself loved," he counseled them. "If you wish to be obeyed, be fathers, not superiors." John Bosco's educational theory rose out of one predominant principle: *The teacher lives to serve the student; not the student to serve the teacher.* In John's view the teacher's responsibility extended not simply beyond the classroom to personal conferences with the student but to the creation of an environment at the oratory characterized by Christian love and joy.

Bosco could make no such demands unless he himself led the way.

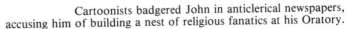

Cartoonists badgered John in anticlerical newspapers, accusing him of building a nest of religious fanatics at his Oratory.

He joined in students' recreation, engaged them in games, challenged them in conversation, joshed and joked with them. A superb athlete until his middle 50's, he would often footrace with them. Although plagued with varicose veins at 54, he could still outrun them. Bosco respected the boys' freedom and carried that respect into every aspect of the oratory's program. If he had to punish, he was careful never to demean or embitter a child.

John never forced any boy to receive the sacraments. There was no regimentation for confession; and at Mass students were not expected to go pew by pew to the altar rail for Communion.

Don Bosco possessed a great educator's skill: he combined authority with liberty, discipline with friendliness, order with room for youthful effervescence.

"Without affection, there is no confidence," he often counseled his faculty. "Without confidence, no education."

Religion for John was no mere adjunct to education. He saw the relationship of man with God as the very source and foundation of all human growth and activity.

For him it was essential to present God as a loving Father to his children. He most effectively did this by being a loving father to his oratory. He urged his students to be aware that they lived in the presence of the heavenly Father who loved them. Once Urban Rattazzi, a top-level anticlerical government administrator who admired Don Bosco, questioned him: "Why cannot the state draw the respect and love of its citizens that you draw from your students?" John responded to Rattazzi: "The force we have is a moral force. The state knows only how to command and punish: we instead appeal to the heart of the young, and our word is the word of Jesus Christ."

In the summer of 1854 the oratory demonstrated both its moral and physical courage. A cholera plague swept through the city carrying off 20 or 30 people each day. For three months the infestation continued. Poor sanitary conditions in the slums furthered the disease's cruel rampage among the poor. Friends and even families quickly abandoned anyone stricken by the disease because of cholera's highly contagious nature. Authorities set up two special hospitals for plague victims. It was a waste. Very few would go near the dying persons for fear of contagion.

Don Bosco called for volunteers at the oratory. Forty young men responded. Armed with little else than trust in their leader, they set forth into Turin's streets and tenements. They searched garrets and cellars for abandoned victims and, discovering them, brought medicine, clean sheets, and, when possible, transported them in wagons to the hospital. Don Bosco carefully organized and deployed his young medical corps. Some nursed at the two epidemic hospitals, others joined the teams searching through the tenements for the abandoned, and still others ran supplies and medicines from the oratory to stricken families. Don Bosco cheerfully pressed every resource the oratory had: its money, its food, its supplies, and its energy, into the fray. Once a young man ran home only to find no sheet for a suffering victim. "Here, take this," commanded Mama Margaret, snatching a linen cloth from a nearby altar.

When in midwinter the epidemic lifted, almost 10 percent of Turin's population was dead. Not one oratory boy contracted the dreaded cholera. More than that, these former street urchins manifested a magnificent courage and charity that won them and their humble leader the respect and admiration of all Turin.

* * * * *

One project almost destroyed John's iron courage. That was his effort to establish a Salesian congregation.

Soon after starting his street work in 1842, Bosco knew he would someday organize a religious congregation. Only men dedicated to the Lord in vows could help his work flourish and endure beyond his death. Thirty-two years elapsed between his original vision and Rome's approval of the rule of the religious society John developed. During his first decade at the oratory he made no fewer than five attempts to initiate the religious congregation. Every one failed. Finally, in 1852, he selected four young men and began to prepare them spiritually for the future. Michael Rua, John's assistant and successor as Superior General, was a member of this pioneer group. When, in May, 1862, 22 young men made their first vows in the religious society, Don Bosco said to them: "We are living in very disturbed times . . . It looks like madness to be founding a new religious society. . . ."

Madness, indeed, it was. In many European countries civil authorities were suppressing religious orders. And the Roman Curia, very much on the defensive, discouraged the establishment of any new religious congregation or society. Indeed, the curia was preparing to consolidate the church's bewildering variety of congregations into a few more manageable groups. Yet it was both the Pope, Pius IX, and Rattazzi, Don Bosco's favorite anticleric, who cleared the worst obstacles out of John's path. Rattazzi cut through the anticlerical legislation. "You will have the support of the state and the king," he promised John, "for your congregation will be a humanitarian institution of the front rank."

In March, 1858, Pius IX, in an audience with John in Rome, was questioning him about his work. "When you die," the Pope inquired, "what

John Bosco and part of his band of "singing, shouting, scabrous slum boys."

will become of your work?" John just happened to have an outline of his plans in his back pocket. As the Pope listened, Bosco pointed out that he would call his group Salesians, since he wished them to be guided by the spirit of the wise, gentle, and patient St. Francis de Sales.

Pius IX, moved by John's sincerity and enthusiasm, advised him to draw up and present the rules of this religious society to the proper Roman authorities. Bosco had no idea that 16 years would pass, of shuttling between Turin and Rome, pleading with and cajoling cardinals, calming the fears of Turin's archbishop (who was convinced that John would take all the vocations from his own archdiocese), beseeching heaven with prayers, and, incidentally, working a few miracles, before he received final Roman approbation for his society's rule. No wonder he wrote in later days: "If, knowing what I know now, I had to start anew all the work the foundation of this society cost me, and to endure all the toil it entailed for me, I don't know if I should have the courage to do it."

Many of John's original recruits came from the poor classes. With marvelous candor he describes these early days of the society:

> . . . our household was not ideal. There was more than one upset. Clerics squabbled among themselves about the work. . . . From time to time I gave a warning here or there, but most of the time I just let things be, where there was no sin against God. If I had tried to root out all these habits with one stroke, I should have had to send away all my boys (from the oratory). A wind of independence was blowing everywhere, which made it difficult to exercise command. . . . With what prudence one had to work! I did my best not to be wanting in it, for I found so many good qualities in these good clerics: they were rather wild and, yet, hard workers, goodhearted, and so straight in their morals. I used to think, when the first fires of youth had died away, they would be invaluable. And I was not mistaken.

What a beautiful appreciation of human nature and an example of patience Don Bosco gives us in that passage. If it was madness to found a religious congregation, thank God for the madness of Don Bosco. Today his Salesian Society is one of the largest groups of religious men in the Catholic Church.

Sister Mary Mazzarello (front, center) foundress of the Salesian Sisters, with a group of nuns leaving for the South American missions.

In 1872 John assisted Mary Mazzarello to establish the Daughters of Mary, Help of Christians. Their work was to be the female counterpart of his own. Their congregation, called the Salesian Sisters, flourishes to this day. John likewise established a lay organization, called his "cooperators," who constitute a Third Order. To this day, Salesian Cooperators, infected by the same enthusiasm, continue to support Salesian work throughout the world. In the less than nine decades since Bosco's death, the church has canonized John Bosco himself, Mary Mazzarello, and John's outstanding pupil, Dominic Savio. Fifteen members of the Salesian family are presently being considered for sainthood.

John worked himself to exhaustion every day, slept a few hours each night, and then in the small morning hours pursued another phase of his apostolate: writing. Drawing upon his prodigious photographic memory, his quiet wit and wisdom, and expressing himself in a clear, direct style, John wrote steadily during 40 years of his life, stopping only when, in his last years, his hands grew paralyzed. During this time he turned out over 130 books, pamphlets, apologetic tracts, plays, biographies, and histories. He published everything from Europe's first Catholic almanac featuring a church calendar, astronomical information, cooking recipes, jokes, poetry, appropriate moral and religious reflections, to a tract designed to help farmers understand the new metric system Italy was then adopting.

Compared to the florid literary style of his day, John's writings are simple and unpretentious. To make sure ordinary people would understand him, he read his works to his mother, or to the maintenance man, or the cook. Should they not grasp any passage, John would patiently rework it.

His writings reflected his personality. He shirked no battle of ideas,

A prolific author, John Bosco wrote over 130 books, pamphlets, tracts and plays.

attacked every foe of the church, but always respected the person of his opponent.

Not all his enemies reciprocated. In 19th-century Italy's tense climate, religious and political enemies frequently used violence to settle their differences. Political and religious foes were not above hiring hoodlums who attempted to mug, stab, and club the articulate Bosco. Once, while John was teaching, a man opened the classroom window and took a pistol shot at the startled professor. The bullet passed through his cassock under the armpit and never touched him. More than once, messages summoned him to a "dying man's" bedside. The patient was bait used to lure him into some dark alley where a welcoming committee would attack him with clubs, pistols, and knives. Once, when trapped in a narrow room, John, covering his head with a chair, saved himself from a fractured skull but almost lost his thumb which a club had laid bare to the bone.

More than once when attacked, John received assistance from a strange, mysterious quarter. A huge, gray mastiff sometimes appeared when John, alone and defenseless, was surrounded by his enemies. The animal, leaping into the fray, biting and snapping, struck terror into assailants' hearts. Where the dog came from or where he went, John did not know. But like some great gray ghost, he appeared when John needed him most.

Only once, as far as we know, did John ever retaliate with physical violence of his own. As he was walking along a lonely road outside Turin one evening, an assassin suddenly rose up out of a drainage ditch and rushed him. Bosco, with all the grace of a matador, sidestepped the rush, and in an early version of a karate chop, clubbed the attacker's rib cage. The mugger tumbled back into the ditch, writhing in pain and howling furiously. John, judging that anyone who could yell that loudly was not seriously injured, continued his journey to Turin in peace.

*   *   *   *   *

"Don Bosco's needs," noted a close friend, "were always greater than the money he received; as soon as he had one penny he pledged himself for two." John not only believed pennies came from heaven but thousands and hundreds of thousands and even millions. He was sure God would always provide the money he needed to serve the poor.

His building of the basilica of Our Lady, Help of Christians at Valdocco is an example of how he operated. Convinced that Mary, whom he had asked to be protectress of all his works, wished him to build this basilica in her honor, John approached Father Rua, his treasurer, to determine the oratory's financial status. "We're broke," groaned the treasurer. The irrepressible Bosco smiled. "Have we ever begun anything with any money in our pockets?" he asked Father Rua. The priest knew enough not to answer. "We have to leave a little room for God," Bosco assured him.

During the building of this huge, magnificent shrine, Bosco somehow always managed to pay his bills. When money did not come from ordinary sources, Don Bosco was quite prepared to beg for it. His begging excursions were almost always marked by humorous incidents. Once, when basilica bills piled high, John visited an extremely wealthy man who had been bedridden for three years. After a few moments of chatting, Don Bosco ordered the man to get his clothes, go

John Bosco's desk.

to the bank, and withdraw the money necessary to pay the basilica's latest bills.

"I can't go to the bank," complained the sick man; "I haven't been out of bed for three years."

"Promise to take your money out of the bank," Don Bosco said, "and Our Lady will take you out of bed."

The man made the promise, then left his bed. John, taking no chances, accompanied him to the bank.

Many people thought John, because of his ability to raise money, was a financial wizard. He was anything but. A wealthy lady, judging him a great financier, asked him where she could best invest her money. Not saying a word, Bosco simply held out his open hands in front of her.

Although millions of dollars passed through his hands, he never kept a penny for himself. Indeed, he lived poorly, going so far as to save half sheets of letters, dyeing string black to use for his shoelaces, and saving wrapping paper and cord. He wore a cast-off military overcoat and used old army blankets on his bed. Because he considered himself a servant and a working man, he cheerfully waited on his boys at table, mended their clothing, washed them, combed and cut their hair. Because he was a poor man he felt hard work was his lot. He gravely warned his Salesian sons that if they should ever lose their love of poverty, it would be a sure sign that the Society "had run its course."

Bosco made many a demand on the Blessed Mother. Once a pastor requested him to give a three-day mission to prepare his people for the feast of the Assumption. The parish, located in a farming area stricken by a terrible and lengthy drought, was suffering bitterly. The farmers were desperate. In his opening sermon Bosco remarked, "Come for these three days, make a good confession, do your best to prepare for a fervent Communion on the feast of the Assumption, and I promise you, in Mary's name, that rain will come to refresh your parched land." After the sermon, the pastor, accusing Bosco of raising false hopes, was furious. He feared that the people would wreak terrible revenge on both him and John when the promised rain did not materialize.

For the next three days the farm folk jammed the church. On the feast of the Assumption, the day of the promised miracle, Bosco awoke and looked into the sky. It was a cloudless blue. The early morning sun was already burning the dusty earth. As John made his way to the church for morning Mass, people crowded around him. "Will it rain?" they demanded. Calmly he responded, "Purify your hearts."

The day wore on, the sky remained like a blue ceramic. As evening came and the people gathered for the last devotion for the feast there was still no sign of rain. As John entered the church for the final evening devotion, he looked once more to the horizon. It was cloudless—almost. A miniscule gray cloud hung like a tiny rag on the porcelain sky.

John made his way to the pulpit. Hundreds of faces turned up to him, and all had written on them the same question, "When is it going to rain?" These wondering, questioning faces could in a short time turn hard and bitter with disappointment and rage. Suddenly yellow lightning stabbed the sky, thunder clapped, and the first heavy raindrops splattered the roof. The farmers, with a new lease on life, broke into heavy cheers and joyful songs. The most relieved man in the district was the pastor.

*　　*　　*　　*　　*

As Don Bosco grew into his sixties, his health became more and more fragile. But he continued his exhausting pace. His days were filled with teaching, counseling, and supervising his endless projects. In 1877 he opened a school for belated vocations. Within seven years the student body numbered 140. This was his last foundation.

By the early 1880's his Salesians had spread beyond the borders of Italy, establishing themselves in France and Spain. He yearned to visit them. Thus, when Pope Leo XIII in 1883 asked him to journey to France to beg funds to complete the construction of the Sacred Heart Basilica in Rome, John cheerfully complied. He could beg for the Pope—and visit his spiritual sons.

Bosco's heart was deeply moved by the warm, enthusiastic welcome the French people gave him. They responded generously to his appeal for the basilica. "Never had such a crowd gathered in Paris around a priest since the visit of Pius VII," one eyewitness recalled. Don Rua, remembering this visit to France, said, "If we had seven secretaries, many letters every evening would still have had to be left unanswered." The journey, however, exacted a terrible toll of John's already fragile health.

John's right eye, injured years earlier in a fall, pained constantly. Phlebitis made his walking so unsteady that two Salesians stood on either side of him. Their presence was necessary, since Bosco would often fall asleep on his feet as he moved through the crowds, greeting and blessing the people.

Three years later Don Bosco made a similar trip to Spain, and he was greeted with the same enthusiasm. He preached from the most famous cathedrals in both France and Spain.

Don Bosco bore all his trials with amazing cheerfulness. Only one disturbed his characteristic calmness. He had not suffered so much since the death of his mother 11 years before. In May, 1867, Roman theologians, annoyed at certain statements Bosco had written concerning St. Peter, questioned his orthodoxy. When Bosco was advised of the charges, tears rolled down his face. He felt his work, already published and distributed, would cause scandal and generate doubts of faith in the hearts and minds of his readers. Fortunately, Roman authorities who controlled the Index of Forbidden Books rejected the theologians' charges. Don Bosco was able to clear up the misunderstanding in the book's next edition. This greatest suffering of his old age was followed by his greatest joy. In November, 1875, his Salesian

Afflicted by phlebitis,
the aged priest used these steps
to get into bed.

sons departed Italy for Patagonia, South America, to pioneer their first foreign mission. (The first North American foundation was in 1892.) Within a short time Salesian missions began their spread throughout the world.

*   *   *   *   *

"You have burnt away your life by working to excess. Your whole constitution is like a coat worn threadbare by too much use. There is no remedy except that we hang this coat in a closet for a while. You must completely rest." Don Bosco had heard his doctor's advice before. The reply was always the same: "Doctor, you know that's the only remedy I cannot take. There's too much work yet to be done." So right up until his very last days Don Bosco, held up on either side by two Salesian companions, journeyed through Turin visiting the poor, begging from the rich, cheering the hearts of those who were sad. He knew death was imminent. "I want to go to heaven," he would say, "for there I shall be able to do the work much better for my children. On earth I can do nothing more for them."

Bosco's doctor now advised Salesian authorities: "He is not dying of any disease; he is like a lamp dying from want of oil."

The famous Bosco humor did not fade. He advised the Salesians who carried him from place to place to "put it on the bill. I'll settle up everything at the end." At one time in bed, gasping for breath, he whispered to a Salesian bending anxiously over him, "Do you know where there is a good bellows-maker?" "Why?" the puzzled Salesian asked. "Because I need a new pair of lungs, that's why!"

The illness dragged on. Don Rua took over the government of the Salesian Society. His first command was to request every Salesian who could possibly do so to come to Turin and bid farewell to their father. From all over, Don Bosco's religious sons came. He had taken many of these little street boys and farmers and helped them to grow to deep love of God. One by one they passed by him to receive his blessing. Next came all the boys who had gone through the oratory at Turin. Hundreds of them came and passed by his bed two by two. John blessed them all, his face calm, almost young.

On the night of January 31, 1888, he turned to Don Rua and said: "Tell my children that I am waiting for them all in Paradise." And with those words one of the 19th century's most magnificent men breathed forth his strong and valiant spirit. During his lifetime he often said he wanted to die poor. Die poor he did. On the day of his death the Turin Oratory, with eight hundred mouths to feed, was penniless. But that did not stop the baker from delivering his bread on schedule. The baker, like everybody else, knew that Don Bosco would find money as he always did, in heaven, to feed his boys on earth.

*　　*　　*　　*　　*

In 1934 Pope Pius XI canonized St. John Bosco as a saint of the Catholic Church.

Don John Bosco, the year before he died.

8. Rose Hawthorne Lathrop

A Home Filled With Love

> The most important news I have to tell you (if you have not already heard it) is that we have another daughter, now about two months old. She is a very bright and healthy child, and neither more nor less handsome than babies generally are. I think I feel more interest in her than I did in the other children at the same age, from the consideration that she is to be the daughter of my age—the comfort (at least, so it is to be hoped) of my declining years.

Nathaniel Hawthorne, the famous American author, was writing in a little red house at Lenox, Massachusetts, informing an old friend in Boston of the birth of Rose Hawthorne on May 3, 1851.

The writer paused, arose from his desk, and walked over to the mullioned window which faced the Housatonic Valley in the Berkshire Mountains. The night was dark. Hawthorne peered outward. Though he could see no more than the silhouette of an old elm, he remained there, deep in thought of the baby sleeping downstairs. What would he and his wife, Sophia, contribute to the infant he had already dubbed "Rosebud"?

Hawthorne hoped he could provide for her financially, now that the sales of his novel *The Scarlet Letter* had brought promise of relief from the difficult economy that had harassed him during the first nine years of his marriage. Vainly he tried to picture Rose as a child of three, of 10. He sought to imagine her, a lovely little creature with flowing auburn hair, scampering over the small lawn in front of his home. Her coloring would be a gift from Sophia. Perhaps Rosebud would also inherit her mother's happy disposition. The baby would be even more fortunate if she received Sophia's simple, uncomplaining acceptance of whatever the day brought to her.

Possibly—he sincerely hoped not—Rose might become heir to his serious, quiet nature; his seemingly preordained role of carrying in his heart the burden of the problems and cares, failings and sins, of the whole human race. Hawthorne turned his face aside, seeking to avoid that intruding, unwanted thought.

The two older Hawthorne children, Una and Julian, were entranced with their new sister. They had lived in a home filled with love; their affection for each other was great, and their feeling for their parents was tremendous. When Rose joined the family, the children expanded their love to include her. As she learned to crawl, and then to walk, and finally to run, her brother and sister found ways to introduce her into their games.

Shortly after the birth of Rose, the family left Lenox and eventually settled in Concord, Massachusetts. It was during this period that Rose's father, Nathaniel Hawthorne, established himself as an American writer of note, and became one of the country's early literary greats.

Whatever Hawthorne's ultimate rank may be as an American author, he was held in almost godlike esteem by his wife and children. This must have pleased him. There can also be no doubt that his family found happiness in their limitless admiration and love for this man. Knowing perfection, or what one considers perfection, involves a high price: there can never be satisfaction with anything less. Rose, and to a lesser degree, Una, were to pay this price. They discovered that the other men who were to enter their lives could not measure up to this paragon they had known as children.

In 1852 the Hawthornes settled in The Wayside, in Concord, Massachusetts, a house that has since become a literary shrine for Americans.

The Wayside, home of the Hawthornes in Concord, Massachusetts, where Rose grew up. Her mother, Sophia, stands in the foreground.

In her earliest youth Rose grew up in a house that knew the footsteps and mighty presences of the founders of American literature: the Alcotts, Ralph Waldo Emerson, Henry Thoreau, the hermit of Walden Pond, and Orestes Brownson. With a loving family atmosphere and great intellectual and artistic stimulation, the Hawthorne home became an ideal background for the formation of Rose's young mind. But life at The Wayside was interrupted in 1853, when President Franklin Pierce sent Nathaniel Hawthorne to be American consul in Liverpool, England.

Crossing the Atlantic to England opened a new chapter and a new world to the Hawthorne family. Upon termination of his services as consul in Liverpool, Nathaniel took the family to Italy. Here occurred a first meeting between the stern puritanical tradition in which the Hawthornes had been raised and the Catholic atmosphere of Italy. The encounter left a profound impression upon Hawthorne and his entire family, and sowed the seeds of the future course of the lives of the Hawthorne children.

There was an interesting little incident during this Roman visit. Rose and her mother were taking a walk through the Vatican gardens, with Rose, as usual, dashing about, peering first at one flower and then another. She bumped suddenly into someone walking toward her. To her surprise and alarm she saw that the person she had hit was the Holy Father himself, strolling about his small domain. Mrs. Hawthorne looked up at her daughter's explosive "Oh!" and came forward to apologize. But Pius IX only smiled at her little girl. He put his thin white hand on the tumbled red curls and gave her his blessing.

Rose could talk of nothing else all the way home. The next day her mother bought her a little medal of the Holy Father and a gold scudo that bore his likeness, and they were put away in Rose's box of treasures.

This period in the Hawthorne family life closed seven years after they had first arrived in England; in 1860 they left Europe to return to The Wayside in Concord.

Rose, Una and Julian entered into the life of Concord happily. Julian began his formal education—he was going on 14. The girls studied at home, devoting their time to the classics, to painting and sketching, and to music. But a cloud of sadness began to spread over this ideal happy family. Nathaniel

Hawthorne's health began to fail. He lost his ability to write, and in one of his letters to his publisher in Boston, talking about something that he was working on at the time, he said: "I shall never finish it . . . I cannot finish it unless a great change comes over me, and if I make too great an effort to do so, it will be my death." Hawthorne died on May 19, 1864. His little "Rosebud" was 13 years old.

But life went on in the Hawthorne family; and the children, bereaved at the loss of the father they loved so much, had to go about the business of growing up.

When the days of formal mourning had passed, the family reentered the social life of Concord. Rose passed through the gazelle stage, rapidly increasing in height until she was taller than her mother. The girl's hair retained its lovely childish hue. Her complexion was the envy of her contemporaries.

Rose entered a school for the first time when she was 14, enrolling in a seminary for young ladies. The school was what would now be called a "progressive" institution. It was here that Rose made her first close friendship, Mary Betts, a student from Stamford, Connecticut. She and Rose shared the dreams of doing something worthwhile when they grew up. Neither one was definite as to just how this would be brought about, or what career might be followed. But there was an atmosphere of liberalism at the seminary, and the girls were inspired by projects for the emancipation of women.

Rose as a child.

Mary and Rose had a second bond: the two girls were religious. The example of Rose's parents had instilled in her a closeness to God. She was not exemplary in church attendance, but God was in her daily life and she was aware of it. The girls often talked of God, of their love for him, and of his love for mankind.

Two bold steps, momentous for the Hawthorne family, were taken in October, 1868. The Wayside was sold, and the Hawthornes left the United States and settled in Dresden, Germany. While living there, their home became the meeting place of traveling Americans. For, after all, this was the family of the famous Nathaniel Hawthorne. One afternoon a young man came to visit Rose's brother, Julian. He was 17-year-old George Lathrop, the son of a New York City physician. He was determined to be a writer. He was handsome, and had the gift of expression which added luster and wit to whatever he said.

Rose was enthralled with George, and as the months wore on she responded to his wit, admired his interest in everything literary, and was captivated by his gracious manner. With such an attentive, lively listener, George was at his best. His conversation was sprinkled with "names" and dotted with humorous little anecdotes. Underlying all was the desire to impress his audience. In this he succeeded and, in so doing, fell helplessly in love with his listener.

There was no question in the mind of either one; they were in love and they would marry as soon as George's writing brought a sufficient income. Sophia offered no objections provided they waited until they were more mature. The Lathrops moved to England, and the Hawthornes soon followed. It was at this time, in England, that Sophia Hawthorne was stricken with pneumonia and, shortly after, died.

Previous to his mother's final illness, Julian, the older brother, had returned to the United States. He urged his sisters to join him there after the death of their mother. But Una, the older sister, announced that she was going to stay in London. George and Rose spent a lot of time together that summer and decided that they would marry and then return to the United States. The two youngsters were married on September 11, 1871.

The bride and groom remained in England three months before sailing for the United States. With their intelligence and refinement, their common interests and a sincere love for each other, the future for the newlyweds seemed cloudless. There were facets of the marriage which might disturb a disinterested observer—the couple's immaturity, Rose's tendency to be headstrong, their precarious financial condition. For Rose and George these were but transitory difficulties which time would correct. George's literary abilities were soon recognized, and he obtained a position as a staff critic on the *Atlantic Monthly;* so they moved to Cambridge, Massachusetts.

In November, 1876, a son was born to the Lathrops. They named him Francis Hawthorne. At this time a shadow began to fall across the marriage. George Lathrop was beginning to show the first signs of the intemperance which would affect both his health and disposition. The little boy, Francis, the delight of Rose's life, grew in age and health. They were again living, at this point, in The Wayside in Concord.

Francis' chief delight was to be lifted up, " 'way up to the big blue sky," and his fond father always humored him; that is, until one day when he returned from Boston and found no smiling face to greet him. Poor Francis lay ill and restless, and his anxious mother was at his bedside. The doctor was summoned and diagnosed the illness as diphtheria. He used the best-known remedies, but to no avail. On February 6, 1881, little Francis died.

The Lathrops moved to New York after the death of Francis, and it was here that Rose became acquainted with Emma Lazarus, the daughter of a wealthy Jewish family. They became close friends, and Emma Lazarus wrote the inscription that is found on the base of the Statue of Liberty.

For quite a while, Rose went without seeing her good friend Emma. After returning to New York from a trip, she heard her name mentioned in a casual conversation. "Poor Emma," someone said, and Rose turned to her companion to ask if Miss Lazarus were ill.

"Why, haven't you heard?" her companion replied. "She is not only ill, but with a terrible disease," and, leaning close to Rose, she whispered, "Cancer!"

*   *   *   *   *

Blackwell's Island in 1890, then the end of the line for the poor.

George Lathrop continued his literary career, but his working habits became sporadic, and Rose was forced to make excuses for broken engagements or to postpone entertaining guests because George was "ill." In public she was the same serene, happy matron, but she grieved in secret. At this time they moved constantly from place to place. Many new starts were made, by George as well as Rose, intent upon saving their marriage from shipwreck.

One of their moves brought them to New London, Connecticut, where they began a serious study of Catholicism, and began to go to Mass with Catholic friends. They were received into the Catholic Church on March 19, 1891, almost 20 years after their marriage in London.

The Lathrops soon became identified with Catholic activities in many parts of the country. They lectured and gave informal talks; they wrote and attended various assemblies. As a Catholic, Rose became more and more devoted to religious services and practices. She attended daily Mass and frequented the sacraments. Among her writings at this time was found a notation: "Asked at the Memorare that my life might be made a willing sacrifice." She began to have conflicts between her religious and domestic duties. A priestly guide told her that a true Christian wife should cheerfully forgo even devotional exercises at times in favor of her husband's well-being. Her diary at this time reveals her solicitude for her husband's welfare, both spiritual and temporal.

The Lathrops still made frequent visits to New York but, for Rose at least, the old mode of life gave way to a change. Part of the time she once spent in social activities was now directed to works of mercy. She was not able to do much, but she endeavored to help the needy by obtaining assistance for them. The dread disease she once heard whispered of her good friend, Emma Lazarus, took on a new and appalling meaning. She conceived a deep concern for the victims of cancer, especially for the poor with this disease. While her friend Emma, with great wealth, died surrounded with the best of care, she saw that the poor of the city were shunned like lepers when they contracted this particular illness. "Could no one be found to care for them?" she often asked. It did not occur to her at the time that she might be the one.

It was at this time that the Lathrops separated as husband and wife. There had been brief intervals before when George and Rose had parted, but the break between them now was final. Life with George had become so unbearable, and even dangerous, that his wife finally applied to the diocesan authorities for permission to leave him.

Though now their home life was rudely shattered, it is evident that the bond of love between them remained the same, and her prayers were to follow her husband not only to the grave, but long afterwards, as notations in her diary give evidence.

When Rose Lathrop left her New London home she had no definite plans for the future, but of one thing she was certain—her former haphazard mode of life was over. The remainder of her days must, in some way, be devoted to others. She confided to a friend: "A married woman, loving children as I do and bereft of them, must, it seems to me, fill the void in her life with works of charity." .Cancer patients in particular were the object of her solicitude, for she found no class of sufferers so greatly in need of compassion and care, none so deplorably neglected. She prayed for guidance, and suddenly St. Vincent de Paul's maxim became the model of her life: "I am for God and the poor."

Rose discovered at this point, to her horror, that the hospitals in New York City would not keep patients suffering from incurable cancer, once the diagnosis of incurability had been reached.

There was only one other recourse for the poor: they could go to Blackwell's Island. That was New York City's last way station for the penniless. There the poor could die in obscurity, and, if one managed to retain a modicum of pride, in ignominy.

"How can anyone. . . , how can we treat suffering people like that?" she thought. "How many of these sufferers there must be! Why doesn't someone do . . . ?" The question soon became, "Why don't I do something about it?" Framing the question took more courage than answering it. Rose knew, at last, what God wanted her to do. She later acknowledged: "A fire was then lighted in my heart, where it still burns. I set my whole being to endeavor to bring consolation to the cancerous poor."

To prepare for this task, she took a three months' course at the New York Cancer Hospital. When the course was over, in a few tiny rooms on the lower East Side of the city, Rose, at the age of 44, began the work which was to occupy the remaining 30 years of her life. She took a flat—the word "apartment" was reserved for more expensive lodgings—which proved to be entirely too small; but the rent was cheap. Best of all, it was in the heart of the very poorest part of the city. Rose sensed that to work among the poor effectively, she had to live among them. Until she could establish a small hospital, she planned to take care of the cancerous poor in their own flats.

Rose had her first patient before she unpacked her bags. Louis Stellar was seven, a Jewish boy, the son of an immigrant. The lad had cancer. Soon there were other outpatients to care for, most of them suffering from cancer, and some just suffering from old age and poverty.

Rose developed two basic premises for her work: the first was that as soon as she had her own home for the cancerous poor, the nursing would be

One of her first humble clinics, the "relief room," where Rose dressed the cancerous sores of her charges.

done by unpaid workers; the second was that if she were to help the poor effectively, she must become as one of them and live as they lived.

While Rose, at this point, continued to nurse patients in their own homes, she took into her tiny dwelling the first of those cancerous poor who had no place to go. Within a short time she was forced to seek larger quarters. Early in 1897 Rose rented four rooms at 668 Water Street and moved her patients to that address.

Each day Rose trudged the city streets, walking from one outpatient to the next, in spite of snow and sleet. Following a stretch of particularly bad weather, she came down with pneumonia. It became the duty of one of her patients, suffering facial disfigurement of cancer, to care for her. Her name was Mrs. Watson.

As the illness continued, Mrs. Watson's strength was sapped. Although the effort involved must have been great, when nightfall came Mrs. Watson inevitably got on her knees at her patient's bedside and recited the rosary. For Rose, the horrible facial disfigurement of Mrs. Watson faded away as the comforting words poured forth: "Holy Mary, Mother of God, pray for us sinners, now and at the hour of our death. Amen."

In order to enlist the aid of the public, Rose sent notices to the newspapers describing her plans and asking for various articles with which to carry on—soft linen and gauze for dressings, medical supplies of all kinds, and money. In addition, she made it known that there was a great need for kindly disposed persons to nurse the sick poor, and she hoped many would be inspired to join her.

One blustery afternoon in December, 1897, a stranger paused before the tenement. Her name was Alice Huber. She was an art student in New York City and a girl of very fine family who had originally come from Louisville, Kentucky. She became Rose's lifelong companion and successor. The two women worked together in love and harmony during almost 30 years. Alice was the stabilizer, the balance wheel which Rose's temperament needed. Both women found contentment in lives of hardship and sacrifice, and each day's work was lightened by the friendship they shared.

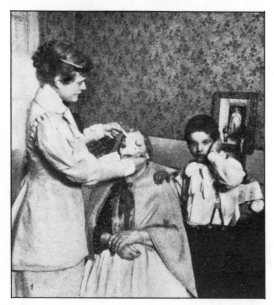

After the breakup with Rose, George Lathrop had remained for a time in New London. They corresponded occasionally. He drank more regularly, and his health failed accordingly. He missed Rose. He loved her. But George was a boy—likeable, talented—and unable to face life; middle-aged and immature; incapable of admitting his own responsibility for the lamentable turn which his promising life had taken.

George died at Roosevelt Hospital in New York City on April 18,

Rose pictured dressing the lesions of the elderly Mrs. Watson.

1898, at 46. Rose had been summoned but arrived after he had expired. She knelt beside his body and offered her prayers—as she had been offering them so many years—that God would take care of the man she had so loved; whom she still loved.

After the death of her husband, Rose Lathrop expressed her intention of adopting some style of religious life and of wearing a distinctive costume. She and Alice even came up with the name, "The Daughters of the Puritans."

In this preliminary habit, which was patterned after the dress of the Pilgrim women, Mrs. Lathrop and Alice Huber went to the New York Chancery. Archbishop Corrigan received them courteously, although he was quite taken aback by their dress. He treated them kindly and suggested that they wait before they started a form of religious life which would be peculiarly their own. Later on, he granted them permission to wear semireligious dress, and eventually he gave his public approval of their charity. Concerned, at this time, less with the formation of a religious community than with the day-to-day burdens of their endless task of serving the cancerous poor, they persevered in the mundane life in the tenement world.

By 1899 a move to larger quarters had become necessary. The four rooms on Water Street could no longer hold the patients who begged to be admitted, and Rose could not turn them away. She bombarded the city's newspaper editors with pleas for help, obtaining enough money to make a substantial payment on a house—a whole house, not just a flat—at 426

Alice Huber, a helper who became Rose's staunch ally and later her successor.

This is probably the last picture of Rose Hawthorne before
she assumed the habit of the Dominicans and became
Mother Alphonsa, the foundress of an order.

Cherry Street. On May 1 the last patient was moved to the Cherry Street building.

With the change of quarters, names were adopted. The two workers became "Servants of Relief for Incurable Cancer." The Cherry Street building became St. Rose's Free Home for Incurable Cancer.

A priest friend of the Home and its charities, Father Clement Thuente, O. P., proposed another change to Rose and Alice. They should become Tertiaries in the Dominican Order. They were, at this point, received into the Dominican Third Order, but as yet they were not permitted to wear the Dominican habit.

On September 14, 1899, Rose Hawthorne Lathrop became Sister Mary Alphonsa, and Alice Huber became Sister Mary Rose. As religious, Sister Alphonsa and Sister Rose added daily meditation to their lives and said the Little Office of the Blessed Virgin. A chapel was built in the Cherry Street tenement, and they had permission to have Mass celebrated once a week.

In the early part of November, 1900, Sister Alphonsa and Sister Rose called on Archbishop Corrigan again and were overjoyed to hear him say, "You have passed through a long, hard novitiate, and I'm going to give you permission to wear the Dominican habit." They professed their first vows on December 8 of that year. As time went on, the number of patients on Cherry Street began to increase, and so did the number who wished to devote themselves to this kind of religious life.

426 Cherry Street, which became St. Rose's Free Home for Incurable Cancer.

Rosary Hill, Hawthorne, N. Y., 1906.

There were three precepts on which Sister Alphonsa based her care. First, the sisters were never to show abhorrence or disgust at the sight of repulsive ugliness brought about by the cancers. Secondly, once a person was declared incurable, the sisters would not permit any patient to be a guinea pig for medical research. No money was to be accepted from the relatives of the patient or even from a former employer. Sister Alphonsa said quite clearly that such acceptance would lead to but one result: the sisters would ultimately be caring for patients who could provide funds indirectly, and the poor would be neglected.

*   *   *   *   *

The Cherry Street Home—and a small flat for male patients which had been rented across the street—were soon outgrown.

Rose Hawthorne Lathrop

The rooms were crowded with cots and beds. The accommodations for sisters and postulants were inadequate. Something had to be done.

Prayer opened the way. Two novenas were made to the Sacred Heart, and on the final day of the second novena came heaven's answer. A French Dominican, a member of a community which owned a large place in Westchester County, some 30 miles from New York, approached Sister Alphonsa about the possibility of the purchase of its monastery. The community had decided to return to France. Sister Alphonsa and Sister Rose boarded the Harlem division of the New York Central Railroad and stopped at the station now called Hawthorne, New York. The religious were led to an enormous frame house, high on a hill. The nine-acre site was beautiful, and the price was reasonable. Sister Alphonsa, envisioning the consolation that this beautiful place would provide for her suffering patients, purchased it.

In June, 1901, Mother Alphonsa (that was her title now) and a few postulants moved to Hawthorne. Within two weeks the first patients were brought up from New York. The new home was given the name "Rosary

St. Rose's Home on Jackson St., the successor to the Cherry St. building.

Rosary Hill in Hawthorne, N.Y., now run by the Daughters of St. Dominic.
Six other facilities are now operated around the country.

Hill." St. Rose's Home continued to operate in the city.

There followed upon those early days at Rosary Hill periods of great consolation, times of strain and worry about finances. But a deep faith and reliance on the providence of God sustained the pioneers. Stories were legion as the years unfolded, and just when times seemed most black somebody or something would turn up to relieve the sisters of their worries and allow the work to continue and to prosper. Mother Alphonsa received help from many quarters: Mark Twain was long a great admirer and proved to be a helpful friend. The New York newspapers and many anonymous benefactors followed Mother Alphonsa's work and seemed to provide what she needed when she was most pressed.

Archbishop Corrigan was one of her most faithful admirers. He had once paid a surprise visit to St. Rose's Home at a time of great need. Bills were piling up and few donations were coming in. As a result, Mother Alphonsa's spirits were at a low ebb. While she was wondering where to turn next, one of the sisters came to say that two priests were in the parlor and would like to see her.

"Who are they?" she asked.

"I don't know, Mother. They would not give their names." She reluctantly went to the parlor. Her visitors proved to be the Archbishop and a companion. The prelate asked for prayers, and as he bade Mother Alphonsa good-by, he put into her hand an envelope so plump and soft that she was startled. It contained enough money to tide the establishment over for many a day.

As the years sped by, the old wooden house in Hawthorne became crammed with patients. The sisters lived with one constant fear: Fire! Two days after Christmas in 1922, their worst fears were realized when a fire broke out in Rosary Hill. Fortunately it was contained, but it brought about the resolution that, as soon as possible, a new fireproof building would be constructed. This was the last great dream and project of Mother Alphonsa. She did not see its final realization, but it stands today a monument to her planning and dreaming and the energetic pursuit of the apostolate that she and Mother Rose shared over the years.

As she approached her 75th birthday, in 1926, Mother Alphonsa's health began to fail. Although to the very end she remained active, the great

Mother Alphonsa was reluctant to have her picture taken after she entered religious life. This was taken near the end of her life.

heart ceased to beat on July 8, 1926.

Among the effects found after her death were several pages of jottings, which give evidence of her constant thought of God.

"If there are any flowers left in the garden of our lives, of selfish enjoyment, let us gather them as a gift to Jesus Christ although he does not beg for them."

"I will obey God anywhere, at any time, with courage!"

"I will see all things only through the presence of God, thus freeing myself of personality and forgetting my existence."

"I will never defend myself, complain of others."

"I will regard creatures in the spirit of Jesus Christ."

There were two pieces of jewelry at Rosary Hill which had belonged to Mother Alphonsa. These she had long since placed on the fingers of the statue of the Infant Jesus in the chapel. One of these offerings was the modest engagement ring which George had given to his lovely auburn-haired pixie fiancee in London 55 years earlier. The other was the slender gold band which he had placed on her finger when the couple were married in 1871.

The legacy of Rose Hawthorne Lathrop is magnificent. Her heirs are the thousands of suffering poor who have been comforted and cared for in the homes which she built in her lifetime, and in the other homes which she inspired and which her community has built since her death. Her heirs are the women who have offered their lives to the succoring of impoverished cancer victims. For each one of Mother Alphonsa's heirs, her bequest is beyond measure.

9. Joseph Cardinal Cardijn

"Cardijn!—Cardijn!—Cardijn!"* The cry first sprang from a small group in the large crowd gathered that memorable Sunday in 1935 in Heysel Stadium, Brussels. One by one, sections of the crowd picked up the cry, and now the name rose in a mighty rhythmic chant from 100,000 throats. The priest who was the object of the throng's attention and affection stood on a speaker's platform in the stadium's center. He lifted his hands to plead for silence. Stomping and cheering, clapping and whistling, the crowd, mostly youngsters in their teens and early twenties, were bursting with a sense of joy and well-being. It was a happy gathering and a proud one. The girls were dressed in simple print dresses and the boys in cheap, neat suits.

They had spent the morning at Mass and, after a parade to Heysel Stadium, had gathered to hear the man who made all the difference in their lives.

Gradually the crowd quieted, and the priest began to speak, at first slowly and gently. Before him lay a carefully prepared manuscript. He never looked at it. He was in deep and complete communication with the thousands

---

* Pronounced car-dine

217

of youngsters surrounding him. He spoke to them of their dignity and how their talents and energy, hopes and dreams benefited their world. Theirs was the world of the factory and workbench, of the mill, and the shop.

Like all workers in the 1930's, these young people were struggling to survive the terrible depression lashing the world. The priest continued to speak and they listened, giving him their minds and hearts. It was an age when persuasive orators like Roosevelt and Churchill, and demagogues like Hitler and Mussolini, moved millions of hearts through the spoken word.

This man spoke, not of war or hatred or fear. With words of hope and love and faith, he challenged his audience to lead Christian lives and to bring Christ to their world. They listened carefully. He was founding father and continuing source of inspiration for the worldwide organization called the Young Christian Workers (YCW), to which the youngsters belonged. This day, delegates from many parts of the globe had gathered in Brussels to observe the YCW's tenth anniversary with Cardijn. The celebration was a high point in the priest's colorful career.

Now concluding his talk, Father Cardijn urged the vast assembly "to be the hope of our times."

"I bless you," he exclaimed. "I send you back to your homes, your places of work, your parts of the world, with one watchword: Conquest!"

This man had nothing less in mind than to conquer the world for Christ. Who was he? Where did he get power to sway young people's hearts? What role did he have in the church? To understand his story and appreciate his magnificent contribution to the modern church, we must journey back to the 1880's in Halle, a quiet Belgian market town, and to a little boy lying awake in his bed at predawn.

*   *   *   *   *

"Come, Joseph, we must deliver this coal before dark!" So Henry Cardijn would urge his ten-year-old son. Henry had always dreamed of having his own business. A few years after Joseph's birth in Brussels (1882), Henry and his wife, Louise, came to Halle and invested their tiny savings in a small and not very lucrative coal business. The hours were long, the work

Joseph Cardijn (third from the left, middle row) among his Halle schoolmates.

was hard. Now, as this day was ending, father and son prepared for one last delivery.

The contrast between the two was marked. Henry was square and stolid and quiet. His son Joseph was small, alert and lively. The coal dust festooning the boy's clothes and blackening his face only intensified his intelligent, snapping dark eyes and the good humor of his puckish grin. The hard work Joseph shared with his father neither dulled his mind nor crushed his naturally buoyant spirits.

A magnificent medieval town hall bordered one side of Halle's town square, and an ancient cathedral shrine to Our Lady, the other. Along the cobblestone square, Halle's craftsmen plied their trades. Cobblers, tailors, bakers and leather workers turned out magnificent products to sell to farmers who came to town for market. The effervescent Joseph loved to chat with the artisans. Their skills fascinated him. And frequently these men would let Joseph work with their tools.

The ever-curious boy, a voracious reader, loved school. He particularly enjoyed adventure stories and listed Jules Verne among his favorite authors. But the stories he loved most of all were the stories his mother told him.

At night, when supper dishes were put away and the homework done, Louise Cardijn would gather her own and many of her neighbors' little children, now in nightclothes, about the large iron kitchen stove. Papa Cardijn would stretch himself on a sofa and pretend sleep. Then Louise would spin her yarns. She told the eager little ones of Little Red Riding Hood, Tom Thumb and Bluebeard. She recited Bible stories. Never did Joseph in all his life hear anyone who could lend color, depth and meaning to a story as Louise did. The sheer power and beauty of her recital so moved the quiet Papa Cardijn that Joseph often saw him lift a finger to remove a tear from his supposedly sleeping eye.

A woman of deep faith, Louise Cardijn's belief in God was at the root of everything she did within and outside her home. If, in later life, Joseph Cardijn dedicated himself to restoring religion to the workingman's everyday life, it was because his mother had lived that way.

Beggars seeking alms from pilgrims at the shrine of the Blessed Virgin frequented Halle's town square during Cardijn's childhood. Leaving

Louise Cardijn.

their home, Louise often gave Joseph a bit of money. "Joseph," she said, "you will meet a beggar. You may either keep this money to purchase ice cream or cake or candy for yourself, or give it to a beggar. The choice is yours." Unfailingly, little Joseph gave the money away. Louise would then say: "Joseph, that's good. Do that all your life." For all his mischievousness and exuberance, Joseph was sensitive to every type of human suffering he encountered. There was one group, however, whose trials affected him so deeply that they shaped the course of his whole life.

* * * * *

He heard these men and women before he saw them. Their sounds penetrated his sleep and sank into his brain, waking him at four or five in the

morning. The little boy would then peer into the dawn's grey light and see them, like so many dark shadows. They were Halle's factory workers.

The shuffling of their wooden shoes against the cobblestone streets was a sound that would haunt Joseph to his grave. The sight of workers dragging their seven- to eight-year-old sons and daughters into the factories, saddened the young man. "Where are the little ones going?" Joseph asked his father and mother. "Places they do not belong," his father replied. "They should not be permitted to work in the factories." Belgian laborers worked a 12- to 14-hour day and earned pennies. Farm animals had a day of rest, but not the workers or their children.

For the children of the poor there was no joy, only hard work.

To this day, former factory hands remember their working days with horror. One lady, old and grey now, recalls that when she was a tiny eight-year-old, her foreman stood her on a box and tied her to a threading machine so she could reach her work and not wander away from it. In the mines, employers often locked children into iron braces at their work place. If the little ones fell asleep on the job, as they sometimes did, they would not fall and suffer severe injury.

Neither politicians nor professors nor, sad to say, church authorities, helped the workers. From time to time a courageous priest would protest and suffer punishment for his pains. Wealthier classes scorned the workers for their drunkenness, endless quarreling and open immorality. More fortunate Belgians failed to grasp that workers saw vice as the only avenue of escape from their brutal lot.

Strikes, of course, occurred. Repression was terrible. Police beat, imprisoned and shot workers. Belgian bishops, judging that their intervention on the workers' behalf would provoke bloody class warfare, did nothing.

One group in all Belgium did rise to the workers' defense—the Socialists. Anticlerical, antichurch, they were the only powerful and dependable protectors the poorer classes knew.

As Joseph grew older he heard of the strikes and demonstrations in the mines and factories. He learned about the women in Halle's artificial silk factory who, half drugged from the ether used to manufacture silk, were prey to all sorts of immorality. Joseph also saw the drunks on the town square. He knew of the family fights. His young heart was already heavy with the pain the workers suffered.

*   *   *   *   *

Now 14, Joseph was completing his final years at the Notre Dame Institute in Halle. His mother and father looked forward to the lad's taking a job. Joseph's extra income would be more than welcome in the Cardijn family. But two years before, the boy had decided to become a priest. Now he had to face the painful matter of informing his work-worn father.

One night, after the children were asleep, Joseph slipped from his bed to the kitchen below, where his father and mother were enjoying a final cup of coffee before retiring. "Papa," he said, "I want to be a priest. I want your permission not to go to work. I want to carry on with school." Henry Cardijn looked steadily at his son and then turned to Louise. "Woman, we have already worked hard, but if we, small folk as we are, could have the joy of giving our son to God, well, we'll work on a bit more."

Joseph never forgot his father's sacrifice. He always felt Henry Cardijn went to an early grave because he took upon himself this extra burden of work for his son's sake.

In the fall of 1897, Joseph entered the minor seminary at Malines. Happy and content, the young seminarian manifested a tremendous aptitude for learning. He couldn't wait for the first holidays to return home and share his joy with his parents and former schoolmates. After a warm welcome at the Cardijn household, Joseph went to visit his friends now at work in the factories, mines and mills. The seminarian's warm smile soon disappeared at the cold and bitter reception his friends gave him. In their eyes he was a "little priest" who had betrayed them

The shrine of Our Lady of Laeken has been a place of pilgrimage since the ninth century. In these streets and this church he began his life's work.

and joined ranks with the very forces the working people felt oppressed them. Joseph's old buddies had connected the capitalists and the church, and nothing the young man said could change their minds. Their rejection wounded the sensitive Cardijn deeply. "It was like," he later remembered, "a knife through my heart."

Joseph was even more troubled to see how a few months in the factories and mines had changed his classmates. In school they had been mischievous but honest young people, intelligent and keen. Factory life was already blunting their minds, blighting their morals, and destroying their sense of personal dignity. Cardijn vowed inwardly to consecrate his priestly life to the workers.

Six years after Joseph began his studies, his father died. As the young man stood by Henry's bedside he once more made a vow: "Father," he declared, "you worked long years for me to become a priest; I will give my life to saving the working classes of the world."

In 1906, three years following Henry's death, Joseph was due for ordination. Seminary authorities were uncertain whether to promote him to the priesthood. "You are too independent," the rector advised him.

Intelligent, dynamic, thoughtful, and indeed independent, Joseph was a born leader. He could be a force for great harm or great good. His evident spirit of prayer and obedience and loyalty to the church finally convinced his superiors that Cardijn was worth the risk. Despite misgivings, Cardinal Mercier ordained him a priest on September 22, 1906.

*   *   *   *   *

Cardinal Desire Mercier, Archbishop of Malines, was a man of vision and courage. Recognizing Joseph's talents and burning desire to serve the workers, Mercier sent him to study social doctrine under Professor Brants of the University of Louvain. Brants was pioneering the Catholic effort to address itself to the sufferings of the working class. The professor urged Joseph to travel throughout Europe to experience firsthand various social programs already functioning on the workers' behalf. Sensing Joseph's talents and aware of the young priest's lack of funds, Brants often paid for Joseph's study trips out of his own pocket.

The money was well spent. Joseph was deeply moved by the energy and sense of sacrifice he met so often among those, particularly socialists and union leaders, who had dedicated themselves to improving the workers' lot. His experience in England, Germany, and France confirmed what his constant studies indicated: that youth was the key to resolving Europe's social question. Within his own lifetime Cardijn would hear another European say, "Give me our youth and I will give you the world." That man was Adolf Hitler.

At the end of Joseph's first year of study, Cardinal Mercier assigned him to teach literature and mathematics at a middle-class boy's secondary school in Basse-Wavre, Belgium.

Although disappointed, Joseph accepted the appointment in a spirit of faith and obedience. He dubbed his new post "a providential misfortune." With customary energy, Father Cardijn threw himself into his teaching. Recognizing his dedication and concern for them, his students admired and loved their new teacher. Joseph made severe demands upon them, but they cheerfully accepted his challenges. The young priest nevertheless felt ill at

Cardijn's house.

ease teaching literature and mathematics to financially secure middle-class boys. His heart continued to ache for the workers.

His assignment's "providential misfortune" gave Joseph one advantage. During long school holidays he continued to journey through Europe, observing various social action programs. He read and stored knowledge for the day when he could engage in his own programs. That day took 12 long years to come.

Finally at Easter, 1912, Cardinal Mercier assigned Father Cardijn to the Royal Parish of Our Lady of Laeken, Brussels, where Dean Coorman

"Together we can conquer the world!" Cardijn told his followers. Pictured is an early pioneer group.

was pastor. According to the custom, which still obtains in Belgium, each priest has his own house in the parish. Louise Cardijn came to set up house-keeping for her son, and Joseph began his work in Laeken.

The tree-lined entrance to the palace of Belgium's king and queen is close by the church of Our Lady of Laeken; thus the title of "The Royal Parish." Sightseers often filled the beautiful gardens that Joseph could view from his front window. One part of "The Royal Parish," however, few tourists visited. Indeed, even parish priests entered there reluctantly. That was Laeken's working-class district, where 13,000 underpaid and overworked factory hands were jammed into crowded and unhealthy tenements.

*   *   *   *   *

It was a damp, cold grey morning, and Father Cardijn was doing what he did every morning since his arrival at Laeken—greeting workers going to the factories. Priests rarely went into Laeken's socialist streets because anti-clericals insulted them and hurled stones on them from tenement roofs. Cardijn, however, had enormous reserves of courage.

Walking beside the laborers, he asked them about their family's health, their jobs, their hopes and dreams. "Are you getting enough to eat? How are the children doing in school? How are things at the factory?" He never asked about their Mass attendance or religious practice. Joseph would have gone right into the factories, but at each gate a sign warned: "Workers only." Father Cardijn was not easily put off. He had already begun to develop plans to bring the Gospel inside factory gates. The workers themselves would be his apostles.

Dean Coorman had put Father Cardijn in charge of the Laeken girls' youth club. Thirty girls of ages 12 to 13 composed the club. The young priest focused all his years of study, travel, and prayer, like a laser beam, in this humble little group. Within a few months, the Laeken girls' club claimed many new members, ranging from 11 years to middle-aged professional women. Cardijn organized the ladies, according to their type or place of employment, into individual groups called "cells," and challenged each cell to Christianize its own world of work. At cell meetings the groups followed a definite and unvarying procedure. First, the girls would consider a particular problem in their own place of employment. Next they would study a Christian social teaching bearing on the problem, and finally the group would read and reflect on a Gospel passage. Then the cell would form a plan of action which provided a Christian solution to the problem. Joseph called this his "Observe, Judge, and Act" plan.

Cardijn always dreamed huge dreams, but one wonders, as he labored in these early days with the young ladies of Laeken, if he could foresee that his "Observe, Judge, and Act" would eventually be translated into countless languages and become a plan of study and action for young workers in all quarters of the globe.

From the very beginning of his work, Joseph limited his role to that of chaplain, or spiritual director, for the groups. He refused to make decisions for them. He forced these young, inexperienced and hesitant girls to make and carry out their own decisions. "They have to be able to do it themselves," he insisted; "they have to fly on their own wings."

Joseph established an intense program of spiritual formation as the root of all study and apostolic activity. His young workers, particularly his leaders, spent much time in prayer, recollection and spiritual retreat. Father Cardijn himself made a holy hour each morning before Mass and beginning his enormously busy day.

Affected by the girls' enthusiasm and rapidly growing success, Fernand Tonnet, a bank clerk, begged Cardijn in 1912 to establish similar units for men. The priest gladly obliged, and within months the Union of Apprentices and the League of Piux X, the new men's groups, numbered 900 members.

Joseph had never been happier. After two and a half years at Laeken, his workers' movement was having great success in restoring a sense of dignity to his parish's poorer classes. Little by little, tenement dwellers returned to regular religious practice. People crowded Cardijn's confessional. A dynamic preacher, he explained the Gospel in terms people understood. He challenged them to bring the Gospel from church into their world. "You are the apostles, you are fishers of men, and only you can bring Christ to your factory, mill or office." He proclaimed this constantly and tirelessly from the Laeken pulpit.

In August, 1914, German armies, aiming to capture Paris, burst across the Belgian plains, wreaking death and frightful destruction all about them.

Joseph mobilized young people and gathered food, medicines, clothing, and fuel for soldiers and families of war victims. In November, 1916, Cardijn, who had worked actively in the underground since the war's start, spoke out publicly against unjust German aggressions and deportation of Belgian workers to German war factories. German military authorities arrested him a month later and sentenced him to 13 months in prison. This

Cardijn was imprisoned during both world wars,
but neither his creative mind nor his energetic spirit could be crushed.

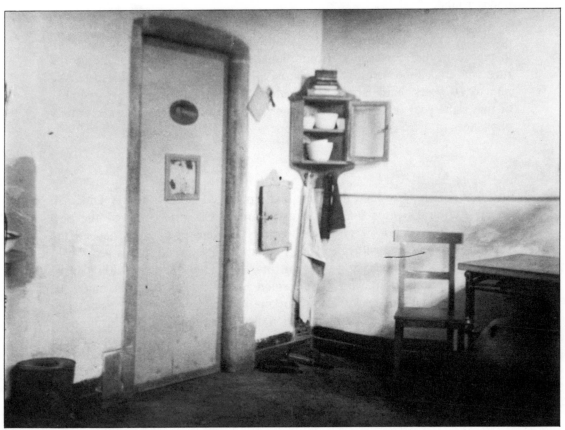

unhappy turn of events proved a cruel blow for Joseph's mother, Louise. Worried about her imprisoned son's always fragile health, Mrs. Cardijn suffered a nervous breakdown from which she never fully recovered. Joseph suffered more deeply from his mother's trials than from any prison experience.

Even in jail, Cardijn made the best of things. "What makes prison bearable," he wrote, "is the passionate desire and ardent hope of getting back to work with a thousand times more enthusiasm than before. . . . Suffering stiffens one's courage in the face of obstacles and difficulties." Joseph used the prison time to analyze and reflect upon his workers' movement and to plan new directions. He read the Bible, Karl Marx, and endless tracts on social conditions. No stranger to espionage, Joseph smuggled out his own writings from prison and in turn received books and material through the underground.

Cardijn had served only half his sentence when the Germans released him. No sooner was he out of jail than he organized a young ladies' group to report on the movements of munitions trains. The invaders broke up the ring, and this time arrested Joseph on an espionage charge and sentenced him to 10 years' hard labor. Fortunately the Armistice came in November of that same year of 1918. Joseph emerged from prison, eager to meet many challenges of a troubled postwar Europe.

*   *   *   *   *

In 1915 Cardinal Mercier had appointed Joseph to be Diocesan Social Action Director for the Brussels area. The priest viewed the new office as a vehicle for carrying his workers' movement to areas beyond the Laeken parish. Now, with war over, Father Cardijn turned to this great task. His innovative methods, however, ran into immediate and unyielding resistance from priests, politicians, businessmen and even Catholic trade unionists. Joseph's technique of encouraging workers to make their own decisions and act upon them frightened the traditionalists. Irritated by the insufferable patronizing attitudes of diocesan authorities, Joseph accused them of squelching the legitimate rights of laborers to participate in the direction and control of their own movements. "You neither know nor trust the workers you profess to serve," Joseph charged.

After several bitter battles, Father Cardijn, unable to sway the regional leadership to his views, moved his headquarters to another place, and split the Brussels Catholic workers' movement right down the middle. With Mercier's permission Joseph continued to organize workers according to his own ideas. Fernand Tonnet, returning from the war, joined with Paul Garcet, another clerk, and Jacques Meert, an ironworker, to assist Cardijn. The trio of laymen, called the "Three Musketeers," pioneered the young workers' movement, officially known as the "Trade Union Youth," with great success throughout the Brussels area.

The grueling job of propagating his movement, the imprisonment, the worry about his mother, and the tension resulting from disagreements with the social action department finally caught up with Joseph in the winter of 1919. Tuberculosis, which had claimed his sister and brother, now struck

Paul Garcet, Fernand Tonnet and Jacques Meert (left to right) helped lay the YCW foundation. Garcet and Tonnet died at Dachau in 1945. Meert survived to inspire a new generation.

him. As a discharged political prisoner, Father Cardijn was sent by the government to its military hospital at Cannes, France.

The separation from his young workers at this critical moment proved a terrible trial of faith for Joseph. A supreme realist, Cardijn knew his political enemies would attack his fledgling flock. He poured out a torrent of advice to his leaders in endless letters. "Don't let anyone discourage you; all those who want to scale the heights must pass through the dark night of trial. . . . Be hard as a diamond and tender as a mother. Call more and more for self-sacrifice, love and commitment."

He begged the Three Musketeers in Brussels to nourish the workers' spiritual life. Warning them to remember that, before all else, they were Christians, he pointed out that their social action was simply an outpouring of Christian love. "Miss no opportunity to make fresh appeals to the workers' spirit of apostolate; it is the spirit that gives life and overflows," he wrote. He warned them not to yield an inch on retaining leadership within the workers' ranks. "It's got to be a real, autonomous union, youth's very own. . . . Don't let any parish priest get any mistaken ideas on this point." After long months of convalescence, health authorities permitted Cardijn to return to Brussels. He came back with a head full of dreams, a heart full of hope and a spirit bursting with energy.

During the ensuing five years, Cardijn remembered: "I plowed through the whole Brussels area . . . through the whole country of Belgium. I spoke despite my weak lungs. I shouted at all the local and regional meetings, to adults, to youths, to committees, general assemblies, retreats, priests' meetings. I came back every night worn out and started out again the following day, and all this in the midst of criticism, intrigue and accusations circulating everywhere. I carried on all the same . . . sure that I was following the call of the good God."

In the midst of all this hard work and suffering, Cardijn suffered the saddest blow of his life. His mother, Louise, age 73, died in 1923. Her loss was irreparable. Even in her illness she had been a tower of strength for him.

If thousands of young workers held Cardijn in deep affection, there were thousands of Belgians who saw him as a madman, a bull in a china shop. In their milder moments his enemies called him a pied piper, a Napoleon, and a communist.

The old guard of Catholic social politicians, who aimed to organize Belgium's laboring class into a single powerful political force, would never forgive Cardijn for establishing his autonomous workers' organization in 1919. Considering Joseph a source of disunity in their ranks, they felt his movement undermined Catholic efforts to develop a united labor front.

Belgian bishops, only too well aware that lay movements could get out of hand, feared losing direct control of the workers' movement, and saw him as a pernicious and dangerous influence. Businessmen thought him a red, a clerical wolf in sheep's clothing. Of all his enemies, however, none were more active, or, strangely enough, respected him more, than the socialists. Up until Cardijn appeared, socialists enjoyed a monopoly on workers' movements. They were not going to let this upstart priest break their stranglehold. Because socialists would strike factories employing the Trade Union Youth, many employers refused to hire Joseph's followers.

Unfortunately, many of Joseph's foes neither appreciated nor understood his goals. His movement indeed had certain social aims. It set out to ensure workers proper apprenticeship and professional training, fair wages, good working conditions, moral protection, the gathering of unemployment funds, and decent housing. But his fundamental purpose was to restore his young people's sense of personal dignity, to awaken in them their true value as brothers and sisters in Christ. He chose to develop the workers spiritually, intellectually, and culturally, and to encourage their apostolic activity. To emphasize his organization's differences from that of the Catholic trade unions, he changed its title from "Trade Union Youths" to "Young Christian Workers" (YCW) in the spring of 1924.

At the Belgium Catholic Youth Association Congress in the fall of 1924, thousands of workers and hundreds of priests joined to determine the orientation of Catholic Action. For the first time, young workers presented themselves as a distinctive unit within the body of the Congress. Twelve hundred delegates claimed the factual existence of the Young Christian Workers movement and chose their leaders. When this issue of the newly entitled YCW came to the floor, the convention crashed into pandemonium. Joseph's young workers began chanting their by now famous cry of "Cardijn!—Cardijn!—Cardijn!"

Young workers delighted to proclaim their newfound solidarity
in songs and pageants.

Young conventioneers cheered loudly and long. Older Catholic leaders and chaplains were furious. They feared that Cardijn's plan to form an autonomous workers' youth movement, if successful, would dry up their source of candidates for the regular Catholic action organization. One priest accused Cardijn and his trade union youth of "carving up the Mystical Body of Christ."

A few days later, Belgian bishops gathered at Cardinal Mercier's office to analyze the explosion Joseph had touched off at the Congress. Cardinal Mercier summoned Joseph to his office and, in the presence of clerical and lay worker movement leaders, accused the priest of destroying Belgian Catholic unity. The charge stunned Cardijn. Although Mercier did not approve of Joseph's methods, the Cardinal had never forbidden him to pioneer his Trade Union Youth or YCW. When Joseph left the Catholic Social

Action department in 1919, Mercier had helped to provide the priest with a new building for his splinter movement's headquarters. But Cardinal Mercier was under tremendous pressure. Belgium's wealthy classes, the political leaders and several influential clergymen were insisting that Mercier burst Joseph's bubble once and for all. Mercier realized that Cardijn was not without support both from the working classes and from some middle- and upper-class people who understood and appreciated his movement. Now, a man in the middle with nowhere to turn, the Cardinal must have thought many times of the pressure seminary authorities had mounted against Joseph's ordination in 1906. Here he was, confronting this priest once again. The Cardinal liked Joseph personally, and suffered much at this turn of events.

But leave it to Joseph to give Cardinal Mercier a perfect "out." The embattled priest suggested that the Cardinal give him permission to visit Rome and put his case before Pope Pius XI. Mercier gladly bucked his headache as high as it could go.

When word spread about Cardijn's proposed Roman visit, his enemies breathed a huge sigh of relief. This unknown Belgian priest, they figured, would never get near the Pope to explain his case. At best he would see the Pope in an audience, kiss his hand, exchange a few pleasantries, and then be dismissed. According to this scenario, Cardijn would then return to Belgium, a defeated man, and wind up a forgotten priest in some country parish. As usual, his foes underestimated Joseph Cardijn.

*   *   *   *   *

"My son, what do you want?" the Pope inquired as the interview began. Cardijn, normally a most courageous man, suddenly lost his nerve and then, boiling with emotion, blurted, "Holy Father, I want to give my life to save the young workers; if need be, I want to die for the working people."

"Finally," the Pope exclaimed, "someone speaks to me of the working classes."

For more than an hour the Pope listened as Joseph carefully explained his movement and its purposes. The Belgian priest was saying things the Pope wanted to hear. As the interview ended, the Pope advised Cardijn, "not only do we bless your movement—we make it our own."

Joseph returned to Brussels with great joy. Cardinal Mercier now approved the Young Christian Workers. His enemies continued to harass him, but not with their former effectiveness. "We are concerned neither with socialism nor with communism," Cardijn responded to these attacks, "but with the souls and destiny of our young workers."

At the 1925 annual bishops' meeting, hierarchy members who had formerly bitterly disapproved Joseph's program, supported it openly. This was the official birthday of the YCW. The movement now took giant strides among Belgium's 600,000 youth workers. By the year's end, the YCW claimed 20,000 boys and girls from the ages of 13-21.

"We are not making a revolution," Joseph told his enthusiastic followers; "we are the revolution!" The revolution aimed, not to reform society but to develop within the hearts of the young Christian workers the realization of their mission in life—to be apostles spreading the Gospel to their working world. Joseph kept the movement's spiritual orientation in the forefront. His youngsters studied the Gospels and the social encyclicals, prayed together, and united in liturgical worship. He challenged them to learn more and more.

"Do people show confidence in your movement?" Pius XI questioned Cardijn during an interview at the Vatican in 1927. "Holy Father," Cardijn replied, "there are still plenty who do not believe in it; priests particularly."

"Very well, come to Rome with your YCW. The Pope will then show everyone what he thinks of working youth and the YCW." Cardijn responded with delight. Ever since his childhood in Halle, Joseph had loved religious demonstrations and processions. Now he had an opportunity to bring worldwide attention to the YCW. Returning to his Brussels headquarters, he announced, "We don't have large financial resources, but we can save what little money we have. We've got to organize this pilgrimage and do it in the best way possible." For two years they worked, and in the fall of 1929 1500 Belgian YCW men entrained for Rome. (The girls had their turn in 1931.) The young men formed processions and attended special workers' Masses in Rome. At their papal audience, each YCW member, dressed in fresh work clothes, carried the tools of his trade. The Pope greeted each one individually and questioned the workers for nearly three

Father Cardijn, inset, speaks to the young Belgian workers on a
pilgrimage to the Coliseum in Rome.

hours about their work and apostolate. "I consider you to be the missionaries
of the church to the world of work," the Pope explained as he bade the YCW
group a reluctant good-bye.

As the Pope promised, the YCW Vatican visit attracted the attention
of many priests and bishops in various countries of the world. The first large
YCW international extension was soon established in France. Then, nation
by nation, continent by continent, the YCW spread through Europe, Africa,
Asia, and the Americas. In 1934, the year before the YCW's 10th anniversary, Joseph had a 40-foot statue of a young worker struck and placed on
the roof of the headquarters in Brussels. This touched off one more chorus
of criticism from his enemies. But for Joseph it was important for people
to see, in the heart of Brussels, a fine building dedicated to the world's young
workers.

After a year's preparation, the YCW held its 10th birthday celebration in Brussels. Priests and bishops joined young worker delegates from
all over Europe, Africa, and Asia. To Cardijn, full of happiness and joy,
this day seemed the pinnacle of his career. Alexis Carrel, the great French
scientist and a friend of Cardijn, wrote him: "Your YCW is a new concept
of life. The success of your organization is one of the great events of our
times."

Throughout Joseph's tumultuous life, moments of deep happiness
always prefaced some vast tragedy. A few years after the anniversary, in the
spring of 1940, the Germans once again invaded Belgium. Just after this
German occupation, Alexis Carrel wrote a last note to Cardijn. "It is of great
importance," the doctor wrote, "that your work continues even in the midst
of chaos, for it is from the midst of chaos that civilization will have to be re-
built. Our only hope in the prodigious catastrophe that has fallen upon us,
is this new flame that burns in our youth."

Now nearly 60 years old, Cardijn threw himself and his YCW into
opposition to the occupation forces. They smuggled young men and women
from forced labor battalions and rescued them from deportation to German
factories. Through clandestine networks he passed Jews and downed Allied
aviators to freedom. Soon the Gestapo arrested Cardijn and several YCW
leaders and administered to them their well-known interrogation. Joseph
underwent several successive grillings during his first few weeks in prison.
The Nazis tossed him into a crowded cell, where he could neither pray, study
nor reflect.

In September, 1942, the Nazis released him from prison, but the
courageous Cardijn refused to leave prison unless others captured with him
were released at the same time. The Nazis threw him out anyway, and within
short order Cardijn was back doing all he could to help the victims of the
brutal occupation.

In August, 1944, the Allies forced the German army to begin its
retreat from Brussels. The Nazis took hostages to protect themselves as they
left. On the morning of September 1, German soldiers burst into YCW
headquarters to take Cardijn hostage. From his chapel Joseph saw the Nazis
before they saw him and slipping out the back door, jumped over a garden

wall and concealed himself in the ruins of a bombed-out house next door. From this hiding place, Cardijn watched German soldiers excitedly scouring YCW headquarters. Frightened because of the Allied forces' imminent arrival, the German soldiers hastened through their fruitless search. As soon as they left, Cardijn, covered with plaster and dust, reappeared. YCW staff members, whose nerves were stretched taut, could not control their laughter at the sight of their chaplain.

But all did not end happily. Fernand Tonnet and Paul Garcet, two of the Three Musketeers, died at Dachau; they had been prisoners since June, 1943. News of their deaths shook Joseph deeply. Hundreds of YCW's died during the war. However, the war and the dispersal of young Belgian workers into forced labor camps helped spread the YCW's message among Dutch, French, Hungarian, Ukrainian, Austrian, and German youths. All the sacrifices, sufferings, experiences and stamina under trial gave fresh impetus to YCW efforts in the postwar world. The last tanks had not yet clanked out of Belgium when Cardijn was already rallying the youth and exploiting the international fervor which the war had unwittingly added to his movement.

Beginning in June, 1946, and continuing on for the following 21 years, Canon Cardijn made no fewer than 24 international journeys. He traveled to any country he could reach to spread the YCW message. Tirelessly he went from meeting to meeting, from school to seminary, to chancery office, to employers. He experienced, especially as he traveled through the

"One of the greatest joys of a man is to communicate the truth that has raised him up, the feeling that grips him, the thrill and emotions with which he trembles."

Third World, the terrible injustice that characterized our postwar civilization. On more than one occasion, Cardijn spoke out against the refusal of the great Western powers to acknowledge the good points in communism and to work out a positive response to its spread. After visiting one South American country, he wrote: "If Pius XII were to go there today and speak his teachings regarding charity and justice for the working people, well, I can assure you he would soon be denounced as a communist and put in prison."

Pope Pius XII in his turn continued to challenge Cardijn and the YCW to witness, before the postwar world and the gradual, inexorable rising tide of communism, the twofold vocation of the YCW—to be workers and Christians.

On the YCW's silver anniversary in 1950, Pope Pius XII honored the YCW movement by consecrating Cardijn a bishop. Colleges and universities throughout the world bestowed honorary doctorates upon him. The humble Belgian priest received civic decorations and became a member of the French Legion of Honor. He accepted these distinctions cheerfully, not for himself but for his movement. By 1950, the YCW was established in no less than 60 countries throughout the world.

*   *   *   *   *

Once in conversation, Cardijn suggested to Pope John XXIII, "It would be good if Your Holiness would prepare a new encyclical on labor."

"Write down your ideas," the Pope responded, "regarding the future development of the working classes." The notes that Cardijn submitted formed the basis of Pope John's 1961 encyclical Mater et Magistra. Pope John also tapped Cardijn's talents and experience for the Second Vatican Council. Two major documents, the Dogmatic Constitution on the Church and the Decree on the Apostolate of the Laity, owe much to Cardijn's genius.

Bishop Cardijn celebrated his 80th birthday in December, 1962. Thousands gathered in Brussels at the Palace of Sports to join in the celebration. The birthday gift that made Joseph happiest, however, was the establishment of the YCW in its 88th country, Madagascar.

Despite his age, Joseph continued his daily punishing schedule. He threw himself into schemes for improving education, combating juvenile delinquency, drug abuse, and alcoholism. He tried to sell Western powers on replacing the military draft with an international peace corps. His vision continued to widen and deepen as he met the world's young workers: black miners in South Africa, Indian banana workers in Nicaragua, street kids in New York, factory workers in Italy. He attempted to pierce the Iron Curtain, but was rebuffed. As the YCW movement grew larger and larger, Cardijn felt more and more the weariness of age, but he continued to drive himself. The long journeys were taking a terrible toll. Finally, in January of 1965, Joseph resigned as the YCW's chief chaplain, and Father Uylenbroeck, a veteran YCW chaplain, took over as chief chaplain. Now Bishop Cardijn could turn his full attention to implementing the decisions of the Second Vatican Council.

A Belgian family gave the building for the YCW international headquarters in Brussels.

Cardijn and Pope John. Cardijn's notes formed the basis for
Pope John's social encyclical, *Mater et Magistra*.

He complained that, as yet, so many segments of the church did not
realize the proper role of the laity. "If the layman is not permitted to assume
his proper role," Cardijn often commented, "the church will completely lose
its grip on Europe."

Two weeks after Joseph retired as international chaplain of the YCW,
Pope Paul VI appointed him Cardinal. The honor created a great personal
crisis for Joseph. "I can't go against my vow to give my whole life to the
working class!" he exclaimed. "Is it the devil who torments me, or is it the
Holy Spirit rousing me?" Cardijn's conscience was set at ease when Pope
Paul advised him, "You are to continue talking on the YCW all over the
world, and now with much more influence." Cardinal Cardijn continued to
travel all over Europe and to plan trips abroad. He was now attempting to
maneuver permission to visit China. After a particularly long lecture series,

a priest questioned him, "Cardinal Cardijn, you must be very tired after all that." The Cardinal smiled and said, "An old man is always tired; but a good priest is never old." He spoke often of death. Like Therese of Lisieux in her beliefs about her afterlife, he was convinced that his work for the world's youth would continue in eternity. A radio commentator once inquired, "What is death for you, Your Eminence?"

Cardijn answered, "It is to carry on living; it is a passover, a transition."

"What will you do in heaven?" the announcer continued.

"Well," Cardijn responded, "the same thing I am doing now—I will work for youth."

In June, 1967, Cardijn was stricken with a kidney ailment. Cardinal Suenens, Archbishop of Brussels, came to the hospital to administer the Sacrament of the Sick to Cardijn. As Cardinal Suenens anointed him, Joseph continued to pray, "I offer all my sufferings for the world's working classes."

After surgeons removed gallstones and kidney stones, Joseph picked up strength, but it was illusory. Suddenly, on July 14, he lapsed into coma. The King of Belgium came, paid him a long and moving visit, but the Cardinal did not recognize him. During the night, agitated and confused, Joseph thought the sister nursing him was a woman of the Red guard who would not let him go to Peking. After a few days' delirium, Joseph surprisingly regained clear consciousness. His thinking cleared and he seemed to be peaceful and tranquil. In his last hours he repeated over and over: "We are at the beginning. We are always at the beginning. All my life God has been so good to me; it is beautiful, it is so beautiful. And what shall we do after all of this?"

On the night of July 24, his nurse felt his pulse and found him peaceful. "Is there anything you need?" she gently inquired. "No, thank you, Sister," he replied. "Everything is right just as it is." Those were Joseph Cardijn's last words on earth.

Cardinal Cardijn still lives on in his YCW, which is presently functioning in 109 countries.

10. St. Therese of Lisieux

Louis Martin loved to fish. Again and again he flicked his rod and cast his line above the sparkling waters of his favorite stream. With graceful and gentle movements he tempted the wily and elusive trout to the bait. Louis' heart was at peace that summer afternoon of 1878 as he stood fishing in a stream near the village of Lisieux, France.

The fisherman was not alone. His little girl sat on the banks of the stream watching him. She was five and adored her father. She had been fishing, too, but grew tired of it. Now she sat, caught up in the summer afternoon's quiet music. The running waters, the humming of the insects, the chirping of tiny birds, all delighted her, but the sight of her father fishing gave her the greatest joy of all.

The sun began to dip. Coolness spread across the flower-strewn meadow. Louis gathered up his rod and reel, and took his daughter by the hand. "Come, my little queen, we must go home."

The fisherman and his little daughter, Therese, walked hand in hand across the fields and up the hill toward their home in Lisieux.

The Martins called their Lisieux home "Les Buissonnets" ("The

245

The dining room at Les Buissonnets was the center
of Martin family life.

Hedges"). This large and comfortable dwelling well satisfied the family's
needs. Louis was a watchmaker by trade, and quite a successful one. He
had also skillfully managed his wife's lace business. But, as with so many
men, Louis' life had not turned out at all the way he had planned.

Born in 1823 into a family of soldiers, Louis spent his early years at
various French military posts. He absorbed the sense of order and discipline
army life engenders. His temperament, deeply influenced by the peculiar
French connection between the mystical and the military, tended toward
things of the spirit.

At 22, young Martin sought to enter religious life at the monastery of the Augustinian Canons of the Great St. Bernard Hospice in the Alps. The blend of courage and charity the monks and their famous dogs manifested in rescuing travelers in Alpine snows appealed powerfully to Louis Martin. Alas, the Abbot insisted the young candidate learn Latin. Louis, whose bravery would have carried him to the heights of the Alps in search of a lost pilgrim, got lost among the peaks and valleys of Latin syntax. His most determined efforts failed. He became ill and dispirited, and abandoned his hopes for the monastic life.

Eventually Monsieur Martin settled down at Alencon, a small city in France, and pursued his watchmaking trade. He loved Alencon. It was a quiet place and he was a quiet man. A lovely trout stream nearby offered Louis the opportunity to pursue his favorite recreation.

Most famous of Alencon's 13,000 inhabitants were its lace makers. French people greatly admired the skill and talent required to produce the exquisite lace known throughout the nation as "Point d' Alencon."

Zelie Guerin was one of Alencon's more talented lace makers. Born into a military family in 1831, Zelie described her childhood and youth as "dismal." Her mother and father showed her little affection. As a young lady she sought unsuccessfully to enter the convent. Zelie turned then to lace making. Richly talented, creative, eager and endowed with common sense, she started her own business and became quite successful. Notable as

Louis Martin's watchmaking and
jewelry shop in Alencon.

Zelie Guerin.

Louis Martin.

these achievements were, Zelie was yet to reveal the depth of strength, faith and courage which she possessed.

*   *   *   *   *

Louis Martin and Zelie Guerin eventually met in Alencon and on July 13, 1858, Louis, 34, and Zelie, 26, married and began their remarkable voyage through life. Within the next 15 years, Zelie bore nine children— seven girls and two boys. "We lived only for them," Zelie wrote; "they were all our happiness."

The Martins' delight in their children turned to shock and sorrow as tragedy relentlessly and mercilessly stalked their little ones. Within three years, Zelie's two baby boys, a five-year-old girl and six-and-a-half-week-old infant girl all died.

Zelie was left numb with sadness. "I haven't a penny's worth of courage," she lamented. But her faith sustained her through these terrible ordeals. In a letter to her sister-in-law who had lost an infant son, Zelie remembered: "When I closed the eyes of my dear little children and buried them, I felt sorrow through and through. . . . People said to me, 'It would have been better never to have had them.' I couldn't stand such language. My children were not lost forever; life is short and full of miseries, and we shall find our little ones again up above."

The Martins' last child was born January 2, 1873. She was a tender plant and doctors feared for the infant's life. The family, so used to death, was preparing for yet another blow. Zelie wrote of her three-month-old girl: "I have no hope of saving her. The poor little thing suffers horribly. . . . It breaks your heart to see her." But the baby girl proved a much tougher plant than anyone realized. She survived the illness. A year later she was a "big baby, browned by the sun." "The baby," Zelie noted, "is full of life, giggles a lot and is a sheer joy to everyone."

Louis and Zelie named her Marie-Francoise-Therese Martin. A century later people would know her as St. Therese and call her the "Little Flower."

*   *   *   *   *

"All my life God surrounded me with love. My first memories are imprinted with the most tender smiles and caresses. . . Those were the sunny years of my childhood." Thus Therese, 21 years later, described her home life at Alencon. "My happy disposition," she added with characteristic candor, "contributed to making my life pleasing."

Death seemed to grant a brief reprieve to the Martin household. Although suffering had left its mark on mother and father, it was not the scar of bitterness. Louis and Zelie had found relief and support in their faith. The series of tragedies had intensified the love of Louis and Zelie Martin for each other. They poured out their affection on their five surviving daughters, Marie, 12, Pauline, 11, Leonie, 9, Celine, 3, and Therese, their newborn.

Therese was the baby and everyone's favorite, especially her mother's. But Zelie was not blind to her baby's faults. Therese was, she wrote, "incredibly stubborn. When she has said no, nothing will make her change her mind. One could put her in the cellar for the whole day."

Therese's candor appeared early and was unusual. The little one would run to her mother and confess: "Mama, I hit Celine once—but I won't do it again."

In another letter Zelie wrote: "You should see the little one using the swing your father installed. It's funny to see her trying to conduct herself as a big girl. . . . When the swing doesn't go fast enough, she cries. We attached her to it with a rope but, in spite of this, I'm still uneasy to see her perched so high."

Little Therese was blond, blue-eyed, affectionate, mischievous, stubborn and alarmingly precocious. She could throw a giant-sized tantrum, and her bubbling laughter could make a gargoyle smile.

In a note Zelie advised her daughter Pauline: "She (Therese) flies into frightful tantrums; when things don't go just right and according to her way of thinking, she rolls on the floor in desperation like one without any hope. There are times when it gets too much for her and she literally chokes. She's a nervous child, but she is very good, very intelligent and remembers everything."

Because she felt no further use for it, Leonie, at the age of 12,

Eleven-year-old Therese (right) and her fifteen-year-old sister Celine, who was her confidante and constant companion.

The porch of the Benedictine Abbey School of Lisieux at the time Therese attended. She was eight when her father enrolled her and her sister Celine as day students.

brought her doll dressmaking kit to six-year-old Celine and two-year-old Therese. Leonie had stuffed the basket full of materials for making new dresses.

"Choose what you wish, little sisters," invited Leonie. Celine took a little ball of wool that pleased her. Therese simply said, "I choose all." She accepted the basket and all its goods without ceremony. The incident revealed Therese's attitude toward life. She never did anything by halves; for her it was always all or nothing.

On Sundays Papa and Mama Martin would take their little daughters on walks. Therese loved the wide open spaces and the beauty of the countryside about Alencon. Frequently the walks tired little Therese and Papa Martin had to carry her home in his arms.

But the idyll was soon to end. The shadow of death once more crept relentlessly over the Martin home.

Zelie Martin, after an illness of 12 years, died of cancer in August, 1877. The heart went out of the Martin home in Alencon.

Shortly after his wife's death, Louis Martin moved his family to Lisieux. He rented a home and named it "Les Buissonnets." Therese was nearly five. She then entered what she termed "the second" and "most painful" period of her life. "My happy disposition completely changed," she remembered. "I became timid and retiring, sensitive to an excessive degree. . . ."

Monsieur Martin and his daughters did all they could to help little Therese who missed her mother so much. They lavished affection and attention upon the motherless child. At Les Buissonnets, under the tutelage of her sisters Marie and Pauline, Therese began her first schooling. Each day

after classes were over she joined her father in his study. Eventually the two would go for a walk. They would visit a different church each day and pray before the Blessed Sacrament. The bond between father and daughter grew stronger and stronger.

"How could I possibly express the tenderness which Papa showered upon his queen?" she later exclaimed.

Inside this precocious little child strange things were happening. To appreciate Therese's interior trials and growth, one must understand one fact. Therese was a child prodigy of the spirit. Her intellectual and spiritual powers were developing at an amazing rate.

At seven years of age, Mozart, the great pianist and composer, made

Louis Martin and his daughters Leonie and Celine a year before he died.

his first concert tour of Europe. At age three, Therese began to refuse nothing, she said, "of what God asks of me." Listen to Therese, five years old, reflect upon her first view of a sunset on the ocean. She was vacationing with the family at the beaches of Trouville.

"In the evening at that moment when the sun seems to bathe itself in the immensity of the waves, leaving a luminous trail behind, I went and sat on a huge rock with Pauline. I contemplated this luminous trail for a long time. It was to me the image of God's grace shedding its light across the path the little white-sailed vessel (Therese herself) had to travel . . . I made the resolution never to wander far away from the path of Jesus in order to travel peacefully toward the eternal shore."

The passage is all the more remarkable because it revealed the theme of exile which dominated her whole life. Therese maintained the first word she learned to read was "heaven." From her childhood she interpreted all her world as only the beginning, only a glimpse of a glorious future. Sundays had tremendous significance. They were days of rest tinged with melancholy because they had to end. It was on a Sunday evening this youngster felt the pang of exile of this earth. "I longed," she explained, "for the everlasting repose of heaven—that never-ending Sunday of the fatherland. . . ."

At this stage Therese gave little outward indication of her intense inward life. She was pretty, and vain enough to be pleased when people remarked on her beauty. The five-year-old had a bad habit of swinging on the arms of chairs. Once a chair slipped out from under her and she landed bottom first in a water bucket "like a chick fills an eggshell." Only with great difficulty did her nurse, Victoire, extricate her.

Therese, given the proper occasion, continued to produce extreme temper tantrums. Following is her own account of one of the more sparkling scenes that took place between herself and poor nurse Victoire. (The emphasis is her own.) "I wanted an inkstand which was on the shelf of the fireplace in the kitchen; being too little to take it down, I very *nicely* asked Victoire to give it to me. But she refused, telling me to get up on a chair. I took a chair without saying a word, but thinking she wasn't too *nice;* wanting to make her feel it, I searched out in my little head what offended me the most. She often called me a 'little brat' when she was annoyed at me and humbled me very much. So *before jumping off* my chair, I turned around with *dignity* and said, 'Victoire, you are a brat!' Then I made my escape leaving Victoire to meditate on the profound statement I had just made. . . . I thought, if Victoire didn't want to stretch her *big arm* to do me a *little service,* she merited the title 'brat.' "

On one bright summer afternoon in 1874 Papa Martin was in Alencon on business. Therese, peering out of an attic window and reveling in the glory of the day, suddenly saw in the garden below the stooped and twisted figure of a man. She froze in terror—it was her father. "Papa, Papa," she cried. Her sister Marie, who was nearby, heard the unmistakable note of panic in Therese's cry and ran to her. The figure in the garden disappeared. Marie assured her it was nothing and told her to forget the whole business. Papa was in Alencon. The vision clung like a sad portent in the corner of Therese's mind for 14 years until God revealed its true meaning.

In October, 1881, Louis enrolled his youngest daughter as a day boarder at Lisieux's Benedictine Abbey. Therese hated the place and described her five years there as the "saddest" of her life. Classes bored her. Because of her intelligence the nuns advanced the eight-year-old to classes for fourteen-year-olds. She was still bored. Her keenness aroused the envy of many fellow pupils, and Therese paid dearly for her academic successes. The ordinary games and dances of other children held little interest for her. She was uncomfortable with most children and seemed to be at ease only with her sisters and very few others.

Of all the Martin girls, Pauline was closest to Therese, her first teacher and an ideal for the little one. Therese thought of her as her second mother. Then one day Pauline told her she was leaving to enter the convent at the Carmelite monastery in Lisieux. Nine-year-old Therese was stunned. Again employing the exile theme, she described her sorrow:

". . . I was about to lose my second mother. Ah, how can I express the anguish of my heart! In one instant I understood what life was; until then I had never seen it so sad, but it appeared to me in all its reality and I saw it was nothing but a continual suffering and separation. I shed bitter tears. . . ."

During the winter following Pauline's entrance into the Carmelite monastery, Therese fell seriously ill. Experts diagnosed her sickness as everything from a nervous breakdown to a kidney infection. She blamed it on the devil. Whatever it was, doctors of her time were unable to either diagnose or treat it. She suffered intensely during this time from constant headaches and insomnia. As the illness pursued its vile course, it racked poor little Therese's body. She had fits of fever and trembling and suffered cruel hallucinations.

Writing of one bout of delirium, she explained: "I was absolutely terrified by everything: my bed seemed to be surrounded by frightful precipices; some nails in the wall of the room took on the appearance of big, black, charred fingers, making me cry out in fear. One day, while Papa was looking at me and smiling, the hat in his hand was suddenly transformed into some indescribable dreadful shape and I showed such great fear that poor Papa left the room sobbing."

Therese claimed she was healed miraculously of this illness when a statue of the Blessed Mother near her bed smiled at her. This occurred in May, 1883.

It was shortly after Pauline's departure that Therese determined to join her at Lisieux's Carmelite convent. She approached the prioress of the monastery and sought entrance. Carefully little Therese explained she wished to enter, not for Pauline's sake, but for Jesus' sake. The prioress advised her to return when she grew up. The candidate was only nine.

During her long illness her resolve to join the Carmelites grew even stronger. "I am convinced that the thought of one day becoming a Carmelite made me live," she declared later.

*   *   *   *   *

After her illness, Therese was more than ever determined to do something great for God and for man. She thought of herself as a new Joan of Arc, dedicated to the rescue not only of France but of the whole world. With unbelievable boldness she stated, "I was born for glory." And thus another great theme of Therese's life manifested itself. She perceived her life's mission as one of salvation for all men. She was to accomplish this by becoming a

Therese holds a representation of Christ as a child and the Christ of the Holy Face.
A month after the picture was taken, she was taken ill and entered the convent infirmary.

saint. She understood that her glory would be hidden from the eyes of man until God wished to reveal it.

At 10 years of age, then, she reaffirmed and clarified her life's goals. She was intelligent enough to realize she could not accomplish them without suffering. What was hidden from her eyes was just how much she would have to endure to win her glory.

Shortly after her First Communion and Confirmation in the spring of 1884, the young Martin girl experienced a peculiarly vicious attack of scruples. She lived in constant fear of sinning; the most abhorrent and absurd thoughts disturbed her peace. She wept often. "You cry so much during your childhood," intimates told her, "you will no longer have tears to shed later on!" Headaches plagued her once more. Louis finally removed her from the Abbey school and provided private tutoring for her. This mental torture continued for a year and a half.

After midnight Mass on Christmas in 1886, the shadow of self-doubt, depression and uncertainty suddenly lifted from Therese, leaving her in possession of a new calm and inner conviction. The third and last period of her life was about to begin. She called it her life's "most beautiful" period.

She was consumed like Jesus with a thirst for souls. Convinced that her prayers and sufferings could bring people to Christ, she boldly asked Jesus to give her some sign that she was right. He did.

In the early summer of 1887, a criminal, Henri Pranzini, was convicted of the murder of two women and a child. He was sentenced to the guillotine. The convicted man, according to newspaper reports, showed no inclination to repent. Therese immediately stormed heaven for Pranzini's conversion. She prayed for weeks and had Mass offered for him. But there was no change in the attitude of the condemned man. The newspaper *La Croix,* in describing Pranzini's execution, noted the man had refused to go to confession. As the executioner was about to put his head onto the guillotine block, however, the unfortunate criminal seized the crucifix a priest offered him and, the newspaper noted, "kissed the sacred wounds three times." Therese read the news with great joy and thanksgiving. She interpreted Pranzini's final act as a sign that Jesus was pleased with her plan to give her life in prayer for sinners.

Marie Martin, the oldest of the family, joined Pauline at the Lisieux Carmel in 1886. Leonie Martin entered the Visitation Convent at Caen the following year. Therese then sought permission from her father to join Marie and Pauline at the Lisieux convent. Louis was probably expecting the request, but it saddened him nevertheless. Three of his girls had already entered religious life. But, characteristically generous, he not only granted Therese's request but worked zealously to have her realize it.

She was not yet 15 when she approached the Carmelite authorities again for permission to enter. Again she was refused. The priest-director advised her to return when she was 21. "Of course," he added, "you can always see the bishop. I am only his delegate." The priest did not realize what kind of girl he was dealing with.

To his dying day Bishop Hugonin of Bayeux never forgot her. She came to his office with her father one rainy day and put her surprising request before him. "You are not yet 15 and you wish this?" the bishop questioned.

"I wished it since the dawn of reason," young Therese declared. Louis' support of her request amazed the bishop. His Excellency had never seen the like of it. "A father as eager to give his child to God," he remarked, "as this child was eager to offer herself to him." Just before the interview, Therese had put up her hair, thinking this would make her look older. This amused the bishop, and he never spoke about Therese in later years without recounting her ploy.

Although charmed by her, Bishop Hugonin did not immediately grant Therese's request. He wanted time to consider it, and advised Therese and Louis that he would write them regarding his decision.

Therese had planned that, if the Bayeux request failed, she would go to the Pope himself. Thus in November, 1887, Monsieur Martin took Therese and Celine to Italy with a group of French pilgrims. Catholics from all over the world were journeying to the Eternal City, to celebrate Leo XIII's Golden Jubilee as a priest. In her autobiography, Therese sketched a charming picture of her travels through southern Europe. In Rome she was enamored of the Colosseum. Its history of Christian martyrdom stirred the very roots of her being. She and Celine, ignoring regulations prohibiting visitors from descending through the ruined structure to the arena floor, sneaked away from the tour group, climbed across barriers and down the ruins to kneel and pray on the Colosseum floor. Gathering up a few stones as relics, they slipped back to the tour. No one, except Papa, noted their absence.

The great day of the audience with Pope Leo XIII came at the end of their week in Rome. Let Therese tell the story in her own words.

"They told us on the Pope's behalf that it was forbidden to speak as this would prolong the audience too much. I turned toward my dear Celine for advice: 'Speak!' she said. A moment later I was at the Holy Father's feet. . . . Lifting tear-filled eyes to his face I cried out: 'Most Holy Father, I have a great favor to ask you! . . . Holy Father, in honor of your jubilee, permit me to enter Carmel at the age of 15.' "

Father Revrony, the leader of the French pilgrimage, stared stonily at this bold little girl, in surprise and displeasure.

"Most Holy Father," the priest said coldly, "this is a child who wants to enter Carmel at the age of 15. The superiors are considering the matter at the moment." "Well, my child," the Holy Father replied, "do what the superiors tell you."

"Resting my hands on his knees," Therese continued, "I made a final effort, saying, 'Oh, Holy Father, if you say yes, everybody will agree.' " He gazed at me steadily speaking these words and stressing each syllable: 'Go—go—you will enter if God wills it.' "

Therese did not want to leave the Holy Father's presence, and the guards had to lift her up and carry her to the door.

On New Year's Day, 1888, the prioress of the Lisieux Carmel advised Therese she would be received into the monastery the following April. She was 15. The only cloud on her horizon was the worsening condition of her father, Louis. Celine remained at Les Buissonnets to care for Louis during his long and final illness. The good father was growing senile. He wandered from his home at Lisieux and was lost for three days. He turned up at Le Havre.

In August, after a series of strokes, Louis became paralyzed. The meaning of Therese's vision in the garden so long ago became apparent. But Louis, rallying his strength, managed to attend the ceremonies of Therese's clothing in the Carmelite habit in January, 1889. The father made one last

Therese portrays Joan of Arc
in a religious play performed for
the nuns in her convent.

visit to the Carmel in May, 1892. He died peacefully two years later. Celine closed the good man's eyes in death. Two months later she joined her three sisters at the Carmel, the fifth daughter to become a nun.

Therese spent the last nine years of her life at the Lisieux Carmel. Her fellow sisters recognized her as a good nun, nothing more. She was conscientious and capable. Sister Therese worked in the sacristy, cleaned the dining room, painted pictures, composed pious playlets for the sisters, wrote poems, and loved the intense community prayer life of the cloister. Superiors appointed her to instruct the novices of the community. Exteriorly there was nothing remarkable about this Carmelite nun.

But interiorly Therese Martin was caught up in an exchange of love with Christ so dynamic and profound that her whole being was transformed. She had every right to say as St. Paul did: "I live, now not I, but Christ lives in me." We would never know about this hidden life except for the fact that her sister, Pauline, who had become prioress of the Lisieux Carmel, ordered her to write her autobiography. The book, called *The Story of a Soul,* was published in 1898, one year after Therese's death. The trickle of two thousand copies that comprised the first printing has since swelled to millions and it has been translated into some 40 languages. Its appeal is universal. The autobiography has captivated men and women of every state and condition of life. It is an astounding document that somehow touches the heart of modern man.

The book reveals Therese Martin. She was a girl and a young woman who was charmingly candid, endowed with a sense of humor, keenly responsive to people and nature, and sensitive. In many ways Therese was unconventional. She did not care for spiritual treatises; she abhorred retreats. She loved the Blessed Mother but could not stand saying the rosary. In an age when frequent Communion was discouraged, she remarked that Christ did not come to the Eucharist to remain in a golden ciborium.

Though all these things are interesting, they do not explain her appeal. Why does she attract modern man? Why is it that many serious thinkers point to her as a "beacon of light" in the darkness of our times?

Love—that is the word. And that is what Therese Martin is all about. From her earliest days she was fascinated by love and determined to plumb its depths regardless of personal cost. She was a genius driven by a ferocious desire to unlock nothing else but the mystery of life itself. "How," she cried out, "can a soul as imperfect as mine aspire to the possession of love?" The key to Therese Martin's personality was determination. And, although imperfect, she was determined to reach out and possess love.

She symbolized herself as a little flower. The symbol was deceptive. Her purpose in using it was to explain that, like a tiny, wild flower in the forest, she survived and indeed flourished through all the seasons of the year, through the warmth of spring and summer as well as the winds and snows of fall and winter. It was her way of saying: "I am a lot stronger than I look. Don't let appearances fool you."

Who was the source of her strength? She claimed it was no one else but Jesus. She interpreted her whole life and all its events as Jesus teaching and revealing himself to her. She made no bones about it; Jesus was her "director."

Jesus watched over her, supported her when her mother died, forgave her sins, instructed her. At times when she needed him most, he was silent; he slept in the boat during the frequent storms that lashed her life.

But without words he taught her the sure path to follow—abandonment. He did not require great deeds, only her love. For her each day was a gift from his hands. Witness this poem she wrote:

> My life is a moment,
>   a passing hour.
> My life is a moment,
>   which flits away from me.
> O my God, you know that
>   for loving you on earth,
>   I have only today.

In this poem she prayed that Christ would be her support for one day at a time, and pleaded for his smile "just for today."

She summed it all up this way: "What does it matter, Lord, if the future is bleak! I cannot pray for tomorrow's needs . . . keep my heart pure, keep me in your shade just for today."

Therese developed her doctrine of abandonment and love at a time when so much of Christianity stressed the fear of God. She bravely flew in the face of religious convention because she could not accept that God would ever reject his children.

Some 600 years before Christ the Hebrew prophet Isaiah spoke of a mysterious servant who would suffer and die but would save all mankind through his pain and death. In chapter 53 of his book in the bible, Isaiah described the appearance of this servant. So disfigured did he look that he seemed no longer human, ". . . without beauty, without majesty we saw him, no looks to attract our eyes; a thing despised and rejected by men, a man of sorrows and familiar with suffering, a man to make people screen their faces; he was despised and we took no account of him."

Isaiah said the servant would be crushed with suffering, but that through this innocent man's wounds we all would be healed. The Gospels developed Isaiah's doctrine and described Christ himself as this "Suffering Servant!" It is in Christ and through Christ's sufferings that God brings his healing to all mankind.

Therese was so moved by this doctrine that she wrote: "I desire that, like the face of Jesus, my face be truly hidden, that no one on earth would know me. I thirsted after suffering and I longed to be forgotten." She soon took for her name in the Carmelite Community, "Sister Therese of the Child Jesus and the Holy Face."

Therese felt that Christ was calling her to participate in the continuation of his redemptive Passion.

Like Christ, she recognized that souls were to be won through the mystery of suffering, and it was to this she dedicated her life. She wanted to love people the way Christ loved them, but she knew this was impossible. And yet this was the commandment that God had given. So, the only way for her to fulfill the commandment would be to let Jesus take possession of her and love through her.

Thus, she had to abandon herself to him. She came before him with all of her faults and failings. She was not put off by them, knowing that he was merciful and would quickly forgive them.

She was aware of her littleness. "It is impossible for me to grow up, so I must bear with myself such as I am with all my imperfections. But I want to seek out a means of going to heaven by a little way, a way that is very straight, very short and totally new."

Therese went on to describe the elevator in the home of a rich person. And she continued: "I wanted to find an elevator which would raise me to Jesus, for I am too small to climb the rough stairway of perfection. I searched then in the Scriptures for some sign of this elevator, the object of my desires, and I read these words coming from the mouth of Eternal Wisdom: 'Whoever is a little one let him come to me.' The elevator which must raise me to heaven is your arms, O Jesus, and for this I have no need to grow up, but rather I have to remain little and become this more and more."

And so she abandoned herself to Jesus and her life became a continual acceptance of the will of the Lord.

The Lord, it seems, did not demand great things of her. But she felt incapable of the tiniest charity, the smallest expression of concern and patience and understanding. So she surrendered her life to Christ with the hope that he would act through her. She again mirrored perfectly the words of

St. Paul, "I can do all things in him who strengthens me." "All things" consisted of almost everything she was called upon to do in the daily grind of life.

*   *   *   *   *

Therese leaned over the wash pool with a group of sisters, laundering handkerchiefs. One of the sisters splashed the hot, dirty water into Therese's face, not once, not twice, but continually. The terrible-tempered Therese was near to throwing one of her best tantrums. But she said nothing. Christ helped her to accept this lack of consideration on the part of her fellow sister. And she found a certain peace.

Again, in the daily grind of convent life, she was moved by her youth-

In the community launderette, Therese, second from the left in the front row, carries a wooden paddle to pound the linens.

ful idealism to help Sister St. Pierre, a crotchety, older nun who refused to let old age keep her from convent activities. Therese tried to help her along the corridors. "You move too fast," the old nun complained. Therese slowed down. "Well, come on," Sister urged. "I don't feel your hand. You have let go of me and I'm going to fall." And as a final judgment, old Sister St. Pierre declared: "I was right when I said you were too young to help me." Therese took it all and managed to smile. This was her "little way."

Another nun made strange, clacking noises in chapel. Perhaps she was either toying with her rosary or was afflicted by ill-fitting dentures. Therese did not say. The clacking really got to the Martin girl. It ground into her brain. Terrible-tempered Therese was pouring sweat in frustration. She tried to shut her ears, but unsuccessfully. So she made a concert out of the clacking and offered it as a prayer to Jesus. "I assure you," she dryly remarked, "that was no prayer of Quiet."

Therese, the great mystic, fell asleep frequently at prayer. She was embarrassed by her inability to remain awake during her hours in chapel with the religious community. Finally, in perhaps her most charming and accurate characterization of the "little way," she noted that, just as parents love their children as much asleep as awake, so God loved her even though she often slept during the time for prayers.

She spoke bravely about wanting to join in Christ's redemptive suffering. In June, 1895, she offered herself to merciful love in an act of complete oblation. God responded by filling her with a happiness, joy and delight in his presence she had never before known. Therese was giving her life for souls. At the urging of her superiors, she united her prayer life and sacrifices and dedicated them to certain missionaries. In the solitude of her cell at Carmel she joined her prayers and her life with their prayers, their work and their life.

*   *   *   *   *

Therese was living in complete union with Christ. But as the last year and a half of her life began, she started to walk a dreadful Way of the Cross. Sometime during the evening and morning hours of Holy Thursday and Good Friday, 1896, the tuberculosis which had afflicted her for the previous two years caused hemorrhaging.

For Therese, the bloodletting was a sign that Christ would soon take her to himself and that her days of exile would soon be over. "I was interiorly persuaded that Jesus, on the anniversary of the day of his own death, wanted to make me his first call. It was like a sweet and distant murmur which was announcing the arrival of the Bridegroom."

For the next year and a half the tuberculosis tortured Therese's body. But this suffering paled in comparison to the mental torture which she had to endure. She began to go into a frightful trial of faith. She described it as a torment, a darkness that blotted out the presence of God in her life. She could find no image of God, her hope of heaven disappeared, her faith weakened and she seemed to be on the verge of breaking.

She wrote:

> The darkness, borrowing the voice of sinners, says to me in mocking tones: "You are dreaming of the light, of a country perfumed by the sweetest scents; you are dreaming of the eternal possession of the Creator of all these marvels; you believe you will go out one day from the fog that surrounds you. Advance, advance, rejoice in death which will give you, not what you have hoped for, but a night still more profound, the night of nothingness."

Therese struggled with the problem that obsesses so many people of our age, the very meaning of life itself. She was stripped of everything—her health, her happiness. She was completely dependent upon others as she was forced by her physical ailment to live the life of an invalid. She was 23 years old. She was mocked by the possibility that all the things she had believed in might be false, that her "little way," like everything else in life, led to a dead end. She was crushed between the desire to find God and the despair of not doing so. She seemed incapable of taking one more step.

The first section of her autobiography was really a dialogue with Christ. In a second section, she boldly dialogued with death. But with brilliance and courage and characteristic Gallic verve, she swept aside death and chose once more her "little way" of abandonment to Christ.

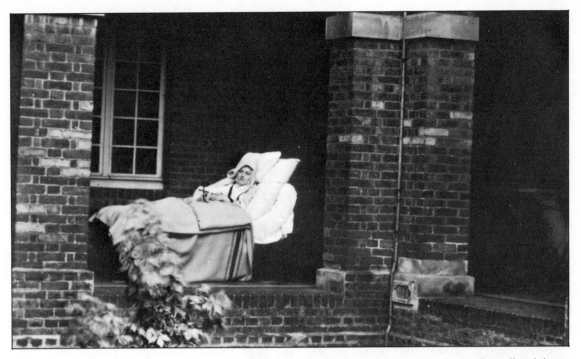

During her last months Therese often rested in the Carmelite cloister. *"I go to him with confidence and love,"* were the last words she wrote.

She was reassured in what she had come to learn through her life, that she was, indeed, the little one whom God, in his mercy, embraced.

She discovered that love is to admit the need of love and to express that need in prayer to love itself, Christ. In this way she found that love could sustain her. Indeed, near the end, she said to her sister Pauline, "I no longer have any great desire except that of loving to the point of dying of love."

Therese teaches us that God puts within us the desire for himself and only he can satisfy that desire. To accept any other source for human happiness leads only to despair.

In July, 1897, Therese was brought to the convent infirmary. She was hemorrhaging continually. At the end of the month she was anointed and in the middle of August received Communion for the last time. Her last agony was frightening.

She had a presentiment that her activity after death would extend far beyond the influence of her autobiography. "How unhappy I shall be in heaven," she said, "if I cannot do little favors on earth for those whom I love."

She indicated that with her death her mission would be about to begin, "my mission of making God loved as I love him, to give my little way to souls. If God answers my request, my heaven will be spent on earth up until the end of the world. Yes, I want to spend my heaven in doing good upon earth."

Her illness reached a horrible climax between August 22 and 27. The tuberculosis had attacked not only her lungs but had infected her whole body. Therese suffered violently with each breath she took. She cried out from the pain. "What a grace to have the faith," she remarked. "If I did not have any faith, I would have inflicted death on myself without a moment's hesitation."

Somehow she survived this terrible time and lasted several more weeks. She retained her sense of humor and gaiety. And yet, she remarked to Pauline that the terrible interior trial of darkness continued. She complained: "Must one love God and the Blessed Virgin so much, and still have thoughts like this?" She saw a black hole in the garden and advised Pauline: "I'm in a hole just like that, soul and body. Ah, yes, what darkness. However, I am at peace."

The end came September 30. Pauline related: "I was all alone with her when, about 4:30 P.M., I guessed by her sudden pallor that her end was approaching. Mother Prioress returned, and very soon the community was reassembled around her bed. She smiled at the sisters, but did not speak until the moment of death . . . it was becoming increasingly difficult for her to breathe, and she uttered involuntary cries when trying to catch her breath."

Therese implored the prioress: "Mother! Isn't it the agony? Am I not going to die?" "Yes, my poor child, it is the agony," she replied, "but God wills perhaps to prolong it for several hours." Therese was holding her crucifix in her hand. Gazing at it, she said, "Oh! I love him." A moment later, "My God, I love you."

Bystanders maintained that her face took on again the appearance it had when she was in full health. She closed her eyes and expired. It was 7:20 P.M. She had written a few months before her death to a missionary who expressed anxiety about her illness: "I am not dying, I am entering into life."

Within a few years, pilgrims began making their way to the grave of Therese to pray. In 1923, Pius XI beatified her and on May 17, 1925, he solemnly canonized her in Rome. If she had lived, she would have been 52 years old the year of her canonization.